The Sourcebook of Contemporary Green Architecture

The Sourcebook of Contemporary Green Architecture

Sergi Costa Duran
Julio Fajardo Herrero

COLLINS DESIGN

An Imprint of HarperCollins Publishers

THE SOURCEBOOK OF CONTEMPORARY GREEN ARCHITECTURE
Copyright © 2010 COLLINS DESIGN and LOFT Publications

HarperCollins books may be purchased for educational, business, or sales promotional use.
For information, please write: Special Markets Department, HarperCollins*Publishers*,
10 East 53rd Street, New York, NY 10022.

First Edition published in 2010 by
Collins Design
An Imprint of HarperCollins*Publishers*
10 East 53rd Street
New York, NY 10022
Tel.: (212) 207-7000
Fax: (212) 207-7654
collinsdesign@harpercollins.com
www.harpercollins.com

Distributed throughout the world by
HarperCollins*Publishers*
10 East 53rd Street
New York, NY 10022
Fax: (212) 207-7654

Packaged by
LOFT Publications
Via Laietana 32, 4° Of. 92
08003 Barcelona, Spain
Tel.: +34 932 688 088
Fax: +34 932 687 073
loft@loftpublications.com
www.loftpublications.com

Editorial coordination:
Simone K. Schleifer

Assistant editorial coordination:
Aitana Lleonart Triquell

Editors:
Sergi Costa Duran, Julio Fajardo

Art director:
Mireia Casanovas Soley

Design and layout coordination:
Claudia Martínez Alonso

Layout:
Ignasi Gracia Blanco, Cristina Simó Perales

Cover design:
María Eugenia Castell Carballo

Library of Congress Control Number: 2010935074
ISBN: 978-0-06-200462-8

Printed in Spain

Index

The evolution of an architecture in balance 9

PUBLIC BUILDINGS 16

CALIFORNIA ACADEMY OF SCIENCES 18
VANCOUVER OLYMPIC / PARALYMPIC CENTRE 26
MANCHESTER CIVIL JUSTICE CENTRE 36
PCITAL – PARQUE CIENTÍFICO Y 44
TECNOLÓGICO AGROALIMENTARIO
HARMONIA 57 52
KIELDER OBSERVATORY 60
SPIJKENISSE PUBLIC LIBRARY 68
GLENEAGLES COMMUNITY CENTRE 74
SIEEB – SINO-ITALIAN ECOLOGICAL AND 84
ENERGY-EFFICIENT BUILDING
AZ-VUB UNIVERSITY HOSPITAL OF BRUSSELS 92
THE MAIN STADIUM 100
FOR THE WORLD GAMES 2009
ALILA VILLAS ULUWATU 106
GARDUCHO BIOLOGICAL STATION 116

CORPORATE 124

HOLCIM OFFICES 126
ROSSIGNOL WORLD HEADQUARTERS 136
NUEVAS BODEGAS PROTOS 148
BAUSPARKASSE WÜSTENROT 158
MANITOBA HYDRO PLACE 168
FREEMAN WEBB BUILDING 176
CHILEXPRESS CORPORATE BUILDING 184
GAES HEADQUARTERS 192
THE NEW YORK TIMES BUILDING 202
BENDIGO BANK HEADQUARTERS 210
WWF NETHERLANDS HEAD OFFICE 220
UNILEVER HEADQUARTERS FOR GERMANY, 228
AUSTRIA, AND SWITZERLAND

RESIDENTIAL COMPLEX 238

SCHLIERBERG RESIDENTIAL COMPLEX 240
HEMICICLO SOLAR 246
LUCIEN ROSE COMPLEX 256
WAKERING ROAD FOYER 266
IRONHORSE 274
LOLOMAS 282
EDEN BIO 290
MOSLER LOFTS 300
AIGUABLAVA HOUSING 308

RESIDENTIAL 316

3716 SPRINGFIELD 318
CLIFF HOUSE 326
THE GANANOQUE LAKE ROAD HOUSE 334
FUJY PROJECT 342
SOLAR HOUSE III 352
GREGÓIRE-OPDEBEECK HOUSE 358
VILLA WELPELOO 364
SENSIBLE HOUSE 374
HANSSEN-HÖPPENER HOUSE 384
OFF-THE-GRID RESIDENCE 392
FLEG DAIKANYAMA 400

PREFABRICATED 408

"DRAGEN" CHILDREN'S HOUSE 410
CAMP WILDALPEN MOUNTAIN RESORT 416
SUSTAINABLE PROTOTYPE: ARTS CENTER 422
BARK STUDIO 428
INFINISKI MANIFESTO HOUSE 434
THE QUIK HOUSE 444
TALIESIN MOD.FAB 452
PALMS HOUSE 460
SOLAR ACTIVE HOUSE 468
NOMADHOME TREND PRIVATE 77C 474
ADRIANCE HOUSE / 12 CONTAINER HOUSE 480
REDONDO BEACH HOUSE 486

LANDSCAPE 494

BALLAST POINT PARK 496
THE HIGH LINE 506
ECOBOULEVARD IN VALLECAS 516
ALEXANDRA ARCH & FOREST WALK 524
QUEENS BOTANICAL GARDEN 534
LONG ISLAND (GREEN) CITY / 540
SILVERCUP STUDIOS GREEN ROOF
HARNES LAGOONING PONDS 550

URBANISM 556

TORONTO LOWER DON LANDS PARK 558
MASDAR CITY CENTER 564
GWANGGYO POWER CENTRE 572
ZIRA ISLAND 576
METROPOL PARASOL 580
VALDESPARTERA ECOCITY 586

Glossary 594
Main International Environmental 597
Certification Programs
Directory 598

The evolution of an architecture in balance

I admit I am a green futures diehard, having joined the consciousness of our time—whether it be as a member of the advocates for healthy food, healthy buildings, climate-positive change, zero waste, zero energy, or better yet zero plus; you name it, I am there! It is hard to get around it these days. It seems as though one cannot pick up a newspaper of any slant and not have our environmental problems staring you in the face. At times, it seems as though everything is in balance: our values, monetary systems, and particularly everything that enables us to interpret the world around us; design in general, design of our buildings, landscapes, and urban forms; because all these things affect us and, importantly, the long term health of the ecosystems around us—our life-support system. It is as though we are on the edge, knowingly or otherwise, headed one direction or another, creating or not creating the icons that might help turn our heads around so we can better face a precarious future.

I admittedly was spoiled. I went to Penn in the '60s, was able to ride the bus up Walnut Street now and then with Louis Kahn, and when I arrived at the university, I was surrounded by a bench of design luminaries arguably unparalleled anywhere: Robert Venturi and Denise Scott Brown, Balkrishna V. Doshi, Aldo Giurgola, Dave Crane, and Robert LeRicolais (the original biomimicry-based structural genius) to name a few. The renegade ecological planner and landscape architect Ian McHarg was across the hall. Bucky Fuller was down the street at the World Game offices, as was one of the country's premiere business schools, Wharton, with a systems-thinking program that would become the forbearer of design thinking and design ecology as we know it today. Students came from all over the world, including the award-winning Italian architect Renzo Piano. Having had the pleasure of working in some of the offices that my professors were partners in, I came to realize that I was experiencing the pinnacle of design and planning, and a quality of provocative discourse that inspires me even today.

So when asked to contribute a foreword to this book, I could not help but be influenced both by my background and by the moment in which we live. Background assumes an excellence in design—no question. The question then becomes, design for what? The "what" needs to go far beyond green roofs and some gardens in the sky, especially since every country, province, state, and city has some kind of green agenda that involves every scale of design—from house to city—and represents, if nothing else, a societal commitment to raise the bar. I am known not only to be critical of checklists as a design tool but, more important, to be a proponent of a quite different framework to support design-planning processes. This criticism of checklists comes from a designer's perspective, not from the usual arguments—too constricting, prescriptive, or checklist mania (although these are issues—but from a more fundamental sense that they, in and of themselves, are not conduits to provoke high-quality design; with some notable exceptions, they do not spark the creative urge to go beyond where we are.

We need a tier of design thinkers who are so incandescent that they transcend green aesthetics and traditional, albeit worthy, ecological, social, and economic thinking; who instill a sense of wonder in the places we occupy so that everyone is touched by and benefits from design genius. It is like sitting down with Louis Kahn at a critique, and in ten minutes the bar gets set so high that you rethink everything. I use the term *architecture of necessity* to describe this—creating profound experiences of place. Very few contemporary designers exhibit this architecture of necessity; fortunately, some do and examples of their work are exhibited in this book.

This six hundred page record of some of the finest work known in the field adds to the legacy previously mentioned a series of new and important buildings and designs that truly represent the moment. BIG, MVRDV, RAU, Mithun, Piano, Foster and Partners, and Édouard François are offices that not only admit the next choices we make are important within our profession and the world at large, but also are willing to tackle issues of environment, culture, and economy straight on, everyday, in practice, in theory, books, manifestos, and, most important, in their work. They have, in some cases, established the mind-set and standard for others. Some have few or no books or manifestos, but those who do are being listened to and the listening is from a public and a clientele who want to join in.

So what do we learn from this book? First, it is important to better recognize what has only been hinted at: that there is a tremendous acceptance by public entities throughout the world to implement green building standards. Just to make certain that the reader realizes the extent of this activity, which I have to say, oddly enough, is hardly referred to by the design offices represented here, these standards have evolved to the point that significant project contracts and awards are often given depending on an office's ability to understand and creatively use these standards. In other words, good design purely from an aesthetic standpoint no longer gets the contract.

Some of the current green certification programs include LEED[1] (US, Canada, India), BREEAM[2] (Canada, UK), CASBEE[3] (Japan), Green Star[4] (Australia), or the indexing systems of Ecological Footprints[5] and the Living Planet Index[6]. In one form or another, these programs are represented consciously or not in the works before you. These evaluation tools presently contain a linear approach toward conserving resources. Recent rating efforts, such as the Living Building Challenge[7] and Integrative Design[8] hint at what might be referred to as beyond balance. The Living Building Challenge takes an interesting step: you must 1) get your rating after the building proves that it works for more than a year, often having to represent net positive water, energy, and air, and 2) perhaps more important, the design is rated as to its ability to engage nature, together with people, to determine the success of the building de-sign. In some sense, these rating systems seem to be now trying to catch up to the quality of some of the work in this book—a kind of healthy dueling back and forth between the standards of environmental performance and the new marks of excellence set by today's design professionals. A successful architect must now reach for more integrative design procedures, where every design solution is never without multiple benefits. This attitude has always existed in the best of architectural practice, but it has never existed to the extent that it does now as part of a combined architecture and engineering renaissance. The architecture in 2010 is not the lone glorified designer; instead it is a collaborative effort that, even though not always admitted to, is the essence of the great architecture of today. Some buildings and even whole city designs stand out in this collection of work for exhibiting these characteristics, includ-ing the Zira Island proposal to Masdar City as well as Ecociudad Valdespartera.

The Sourcebook of Contemporary Green Architecture, by emphasizing the pictorial and therefore mostly the aesthetic and not concentrating on either the theory behind a building nor a successful rating determined by green certifica-tion, takes an interesting stance. The book essentially asks if people respond on a primary level—in other words, are they engaged by a visceral sense of color, shape, spatial character, and material texture. Of course if you cannot get that level of connection, the rest might not actually ever be entered into, due to the lack of any interest to get to the next level by the user or the public.

Many buildings that particularly stood out due to this visceral level of understanding in the design sense also offered in-depth environmental rigor. Vice versa, in other cases, this depth did exist while the aesthetics were in question. A building that contains places for birds and even bats to nest in its walls might automatically be categorized as not up to modern architectural standards and might instead be regarded as some medieval aberration. Yet the WWF Headquarters by RAU Architects did just this (creating habitat for birds and bats) and succeeded, in my estimation, on nearly all fronts, at least from what one can see. Another, by Triptyque was a pure architectural delight but probably could not have pulled together its particular aesthetics without using the principles of green walls now in vogue with several of the architects found in this book. The part that stands out perhaps better than any other is the unusual playfulness between nature and technology. Both seem to need each other. Then, of course, there is provocative green which fills the viewer with a level of amazement seldom experienced in a building or landscape. Wastewater

treatment made into art and buildings such as the Queens Botanical Gardens brings water purification to a new level, while the green facades of Edouard François'Eden Bio and his French rival, Patrick Blanc[9], who unfortunately does not appear in this series, create buildings literally as living systems for people and nature.

So what will be next? In other words, what should we expect to see ten years from now or, from my perspective, what should we be finding beyond just the visual, quasiorganic architecture where we really involve ourselves with the metabolism of the building. Examples where structural failure brought into the area of self-repair by mimicking how bones in the body heal by attracting tiny electrical currents to the fracture points have been mimicked in a sea-based architecture, similar to coral reef growing, in what was called Biorock. Buildings that create interaction between nature and humans is not a new idea (see Wolf Hilbertz's discussions on Cybertecture[10] in the '70s and '80s). Structures that are created or dissipated, depending on human spatial and psychological needs, have also been attempted. But this was all done with computer interfaces, not directly between brain and building but almost. Today, twenty-five years later, the brain is being connected directly in a manner that can control a buildings mechanical system and protective skin in response to human need. Perhaps an *Avatar* architecture is soon in the making.

It seems that with the precarious position the world sits in, we must get closer to nature's wisdom. The cycles around us are what matters, whether we choose to be part of this continuum is at stake. Are we to remain in an open, cooperative relationship with nature, able to continue to learn from each other, or are we destined to go our own way and forget the millennia of wisdom that supports our every move?

Pliny Fisk III

Pliny Fisk III is codirector and cofounder of the oldest nonprofit in the United States focusing on sustainable architecture and planning, the Center for Maximum Potential Building Systems in Austin, Texas. CMPBS focuses on all aspects of sustainability, with work applied at the local, state, and national levels. As designers, planners, and policy makers, the organization has been at the forefront of green design for more than three decades. Pliny has been referred to as one of the United States' most important futurists and ecopioneers by *Metropolis Magazine*, *Architecture* magazine and *Architectural Record*.

Pliny is also signature faculty in Architecture, Landscape Architecture, and Planning at Texas A&M University, where he is a fellow in Sustainable Urbanism, a fellow in Health Systems Design, and a fellow at the Center for Housing and Urban Development.

www.cmpbs.org

Further interesting movements: Biomimicry[A], Biophilia[B], the Living Building Challenge[C], Permaculture[D], Integrative Design[E], Excursions on Capacity KM3[F], Metacity/Datatown[G], Yes is More[H], Superuse[I].

Further reading:

A. Benyus, Janine M. *Biomimicry: Innovation Inspired by Nature*. New York: William Morrow & Company, Inc., 1997.

B. Kellert, Stephen R., Judith Heerwagen, and Martin Mador. *Biophilic Design: The Theory, Science and Practice of Bringing Buildings to Life*. New Jersey: John Wiley and Sons, 2008.

C. www.ilbi.org

D. Mollison, Bill. *Permaculture: A Designers' Manual*. Tasmania: Tagari Publications, 1988.

E. 7 Group, and Bill Reed. *The Integrative Design Guide to Green Building*. New Jersey: John Wiley and Sons, 2009.

F. MVRDV. *MVRDV: KM3: Excursions on Capacity*. Barcelona: Actar, 2006.

G. MVRDV. *Metacity/Datatown*. Rotterdam: MVRDV/010 Publishers, 1999.

H. Ingels, Bjarke. *Yes Is More: An Archicomic on Architectural Evolution*. Cologne: Evergreen-Taschen, 2009.

I. Jongert, Jan, Cesare Peeren, and Ed van Hinte, eds. *Superuse: Constructing New Architecture by Shortcutting Material Flows*. Rotterdam: 010 Publishers, 2007.

Footnotes:

1. www.usgbc.org/leed
2. www.breeam.org
3. www.ibec.or.jp/CASBEE
4. www.gbca.org.au/green-star
5. www.footprintnetwork.org
6. www.panda.org/about_our_earth/all_publications/living_planet_report/
7. www.ilbi.org
8. 7 Group and Bill Reed. *The Integrative Design Guide to Green Building*. New Jersey: John Wiley and Sons, 2009.
9. Blanc, Patrick and Veronique Lalot. *The Vertical Garden: From Nature to the City*. New York: W. W. Norton and Company, 2008.
10. www.wolfhilbertz.com

PUBLIC BUILDINGS

CALIFORNIA ACADEMY OF SCIENCES

San Francisco, CA, USA   2008

The new California Academy of Sciences is one of the few natural science institutes to combine public exhibits with scientific research. The private area of this academy has existed since its foundation. However, the aim of its renovation was to provide exhibition space and an educational facility accessible by the public.

The new building for this scientific and cultural center is on the original location, in Golden Gate Park, although it required the demolition of eleven older buildings dating from between 1916 to 1976. The different areas are laid out around a large central atrium. The roof holds 55,000 photovoltaic cells that cover the power requirements for the entire complex.

The predominant building materials are natural stone (limestone), gray concrete (facades and outer walls), steel, and glass. The structural frame is made from reinforced concrete, complemented by concrete floors and shear walls, and a steel roof. Neutral colors are used in keeping with the building's iconic status.

The environmental strategies of the project concerned its efficient heating-cooling system and the reuse of materials from the demolition of the old buildings. The building has a high interior air quality. The space devoted to research and administration is provided with natural ventilation and lighting through the use of regulable louvers and automatic sunshades that control the amount of sunlight entering the building. Water is collected on the roof, where plants adapted to dry conditions have been planted and the photovoltaic panels are located.

ARCHITECT
Renzo Piano Building Workshop

CLIENT
California Academy of Sciences

COLLABORATORS
Stantec Architecture, Ove Arup & Partners (engineering and sustainability), Rutherford & Chekene (civil engineering), SWA Group (landscaping), Rana Creek (green roof), PBS&J (aquarium support systems), Thinc Design, Cinnabar, Visual-Acuity (exhibitions)

TOTAL SURFACE AREA
410,000 sq ft

COST
USD 370,000,000 (includes exhibition program and costs arising from temporary location)

CERTIFICATION
USGBC LEED platinum

PROGRAM
Building with public areas (classrooms, auditorium, aquarium, and temporary exhibition space) and private areas (research, administration, library, and storage)

Photography © Tim Griffith, Tom Fox

This seemingly lightweight structure blends
seamlessly with the existing parkland. This academy is
one of the world's greenest museums, having scored a
total of 54 points in its LEED certification audit.

Longitudinal elevation

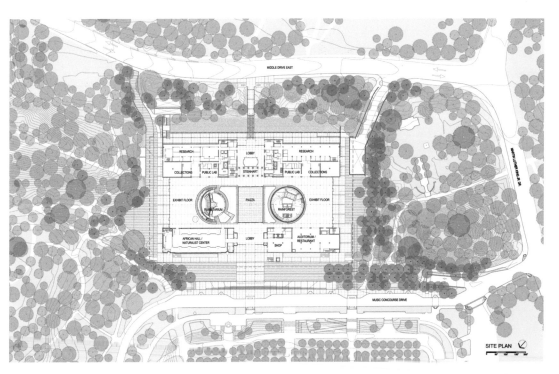

Site plan

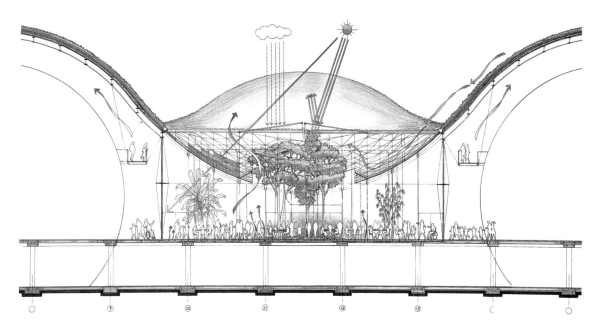

Rendering of the central atrium, with bioclimatic parameters.

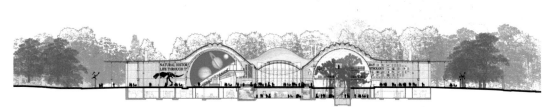

Cross-section through planetarium and tropical rainforest.

90% of the interior spaces receive natural lighting during the day. The central atrium, a social meeting point, has regulable skylights in its roof to provide ventilation and natural light.

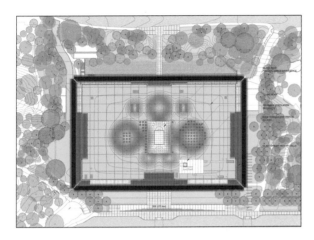

Roof plan

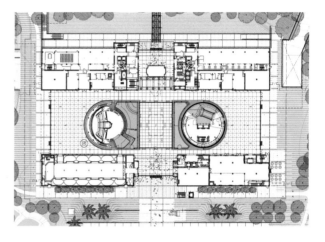

Ground plan of public areas

VANCOUVER OLYMPIC / PARALYMPIC CENTRE

Vancouver, British Columbia, Canada   2010

This facility, with capacity for six thousand people, was initially built to host curling competitions during the Vancouver Winter Olympic and Paralympic Games, but was also planned for future use as a recreational and multipurpose community center. It features a gym, multipurpose spaces, aerobics rooms, a fitness center, and before- and after-school child care facilities. There is also an ice rink, curling club, library, and an adjacent 66,700 sq ft aquatic center with an Olympic-size pool and other leisure pools.

The program took into account the use for the curling competition during the 2010 Winter Olympics and Paralympics as well as future uses of the facility for other events.

The design incorporates programs for water capture, heat gain enhancement, natural lighting, use of FSC-certified wood products, and low-VOC materials.

Heat is captured by mechanical systems. The heat left over from refrigeration of the ice rink is used to heat the building, the aquatic center, and the future community center, and to run the air-conditioning system, increasing energy efficiency by 40% compared to a standard building not intended for LEED certification.

During the Olympics, the ventilation, cooling, and dehumidifying systems were controlled online to adjust for foreseeable ice melting, owing to the effect of having thousands of spectators.

ARCHITECT
Hughes Condon Marler Architects

CLIENT
Vancouver Organizing Committee

TOTAL SURFACE AREA
173,000 sq ft

COST
USD 85,450,000

ENERGY CONSUMPTION
41 kWh/sq ft/year

CERTIFICATION
USGBC LEED gold—pending

PROGRAM
Community facility with sporting area, after-school activities, and arts and crafts room

Photography © Hubert Kang

The facility is currently in the process of LEED Gold certification, the highest level rating given by the U.S. Green Building Council (USGBC). BC Hydro monitored its energy use during the Olympics. Information is available at www.venueenergytracker.com.

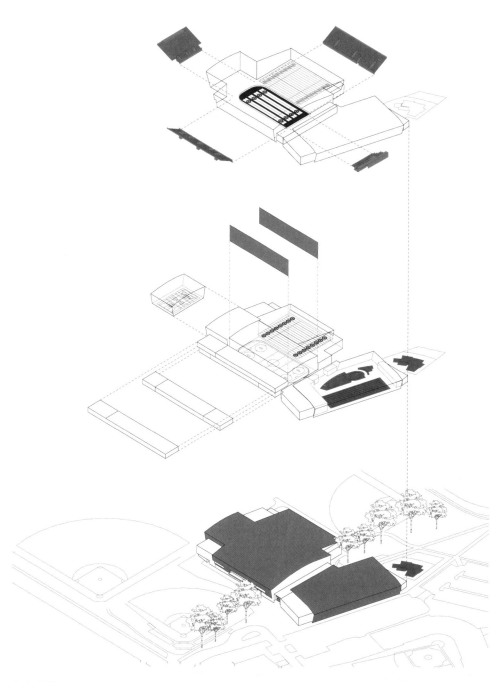

Exploded isometric view

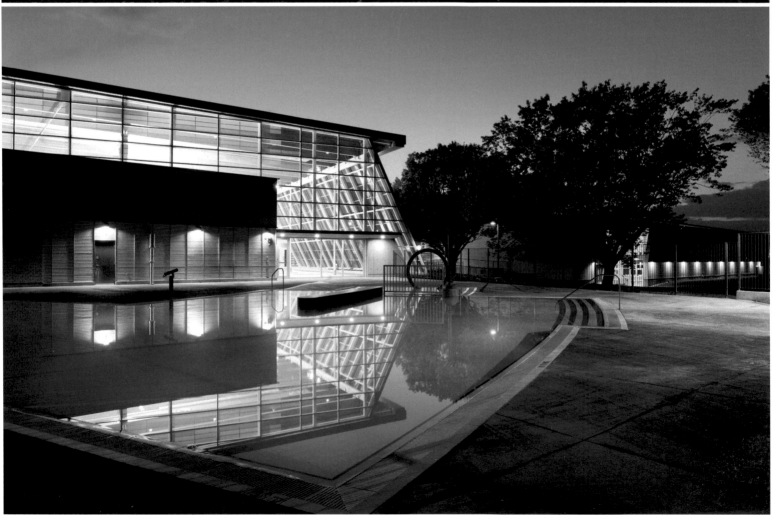

North elevation

East elevation

South elevation

West elevation

The heat-recovery system that connects the ice rink with the swimming pool is of great importance in reducing the facility's carbon footprint. This system supplies heat to the leisure pools, showers, and ventilation system.

Ground plan

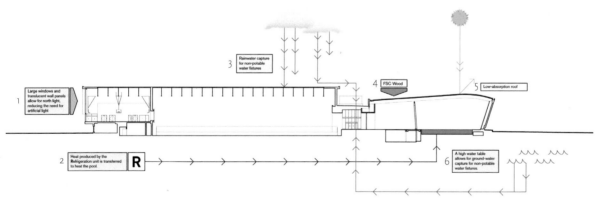

Diagram with bioclimatic features

1. Glazing on north facade to enhance natural lighting
2. The heat from the refrigeration system is transferred to the pools
3. Water capture for use with nonpotable fixtures
4. FSC-certified wood
5. Low-radiation-absorption roof
6. Water table providing water for nonpotable fixtures

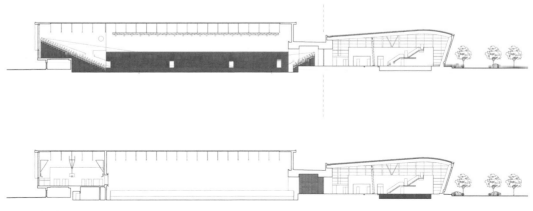

Longitudinal section

MANCHESTER CIVIL JUSTICE CENTRE

Manchester, United Kingdom   2008

Manchester's central court complex is a fifteen-story building containing courts and offices. Its north and south facades are designed in stratified layers. It is the largest court complex that has been built in England since the Royal Courts of Justice were constructed in 1882 in London.

One of the requirements of its design was that the building should have minimum impact in its energy use. One of the steps for fulfilling this aim was the integration of passive energy systems within the morphology of the building to modify the internal climate and reduce energy demand for air-conditioning systems. Passive design needs little technology and is low maintenance. Following these guidelines, the architects chose to accentuate natural ventilation as the air-conditioning component in substitution of mechanical heating and cooling systems. Comfort conditions are achieved in spring and summer by introducing air from outside through vents and under-floor chambers.

The courts are designed to operate with natural ventilation 63% of the year and 100% of the time from May through October. The use of a groundwater cooling system reduces electricity consumption for this task by one third. Water is drawn from an aquifer 330 ft below the site and is pumped by means of a heat exchanger, improving efficiency by 15%.

ARCHITECT
Denton Corker Marshall

CLIENT
Allied London Properties/UK Government Courts Service

COLLABORATORS
Adrian FitzGerald (associate architect), Allied London Properties (developer), Mott MacDonald (structural and services consultant), Gardiner and Theobald (measurements and materials calculation), Bovis Lend Lease (builder)

SURFACE AREA
366,000 sq ft

COST
USD 18,500,000

CERTIFICATION
BREEAM Excellent

PROGRAM
New court complex in Manchester

Photography © Tim Griffith, Paul Riddle, Morley Von Sternberg, Daniel Hopkinson

One of the conditions of the project was that the
building could be turned into an office block in a space
of thirty-five years to extend its useful life.

Rendering

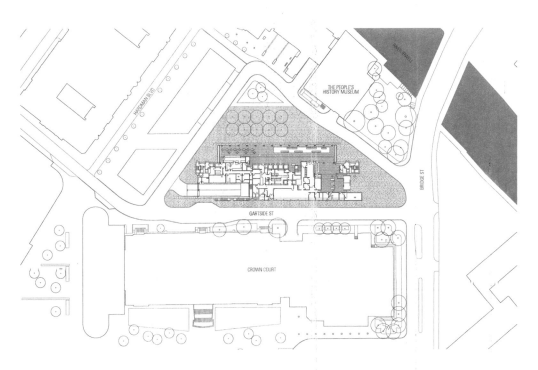

Site plan

A double-skin facade provides ventilation, protection from the sun, and abundant entry of light. The finishes and materials used on the exterior and in the interior of the building were chosen for their durability, sustainability, and low maintenance.

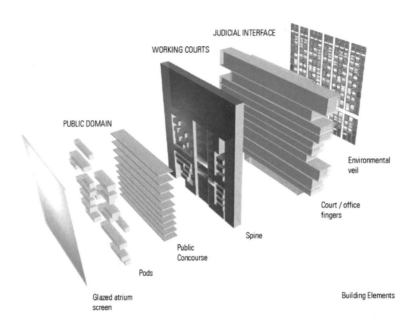

Exploded diagram of the building

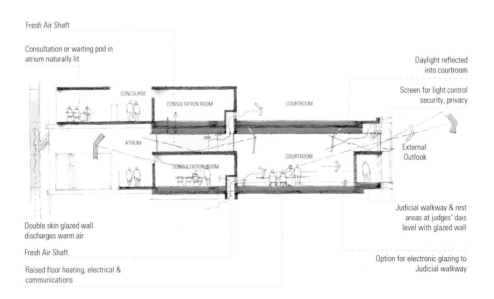

Section with environmental features

PCITAL – PARQUE CIENTÍFICO Y TECNOLÓGICO AGROALIMENTARIO

Lleida, Spain   2009

The existing buildings in this complex in the Gardeny district are a good example of architecture indebted to the first rationalist movement, with a language akin to art deco and expressionism. The architectural proposal consisted of restoring three former army barracks buildings in the city of Lleida and converting them into large multipurpose spaces, including offices and facilities for agrifood research and innovation.

The positives of the six existing linear volumes, interconnected with flexible floor plans and open to changed uses, are reinforced and maintained. The buildings were developed into a single unit by covering the courtyards between them with modular greenhouse canopies inspired by the world of agricultural innovation, and enabling a thermal space to be created.

The facades of the old buildings facing the courtyards were respected—the textures, colors, and ornamentation were restored—and only the louvers that protect direct sunlight from hitting the building break with its original design.

The high inertia of the existing buildings was reinforced and the outer walls were insulated in order to take advantage of the accumulation of heat and cool on the inside.

Low-environmental impact and highly recyclable materials were used. The building makes use of rainwater through green cistern roofs, in addition to water produced by external condensation of the abundant fog occurring in the Lleida area. The end result: energy savings of 51% are achieved compared to conventional buildings.

ARCHITECT
Equip d'Arquitectura Pich-Aguilera

CLIENT
Consorcio del Parque Científico Tecnológico Agroalimentario (PCiTAL)

COLLABORATORS
Boma-Sala (structural consultant), EINESA (engineering), Societat Orgànica (energy consultant), Beegroupcimne – ITL – Grup Energia Solar UDL (energy control monitoring), Felip Solsona (quantity surveyor)

TOTAL SURFACE AREA
204,700 sq ft

COST
USD 12,767,000

ENERGY CONSUMPTION
0.10 kWh/sq ft/year (heating), 6.5 kWh/ sq ft/year (cooling)

PROGRAM
Offices and facilities for university and agrifood company research

Photography © Jordi V. Pou

Each courtyard is designed with color and vegetation.
The greenhouse canopy roof is opened in summer and
functions as a natural flue to create cross-ventilation.

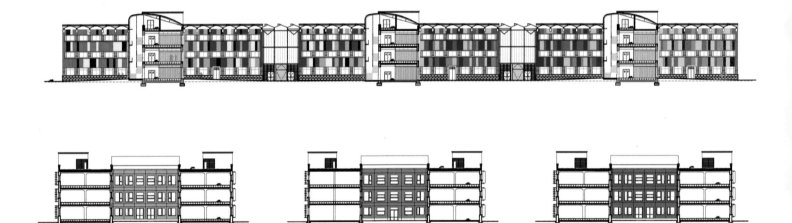

Sections of courtyards with colors

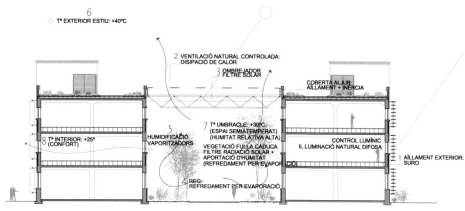

Bioclimatic diagram (summer)

1. Exterior insulation (cork)
2. Controlled natural ventilation: heat dissipation
3. Sunshades
4. Evapotranspiration
5. Humidifiers
6. Exterior temperature: 104 °F
7. Courtyard temperature: 86 °F
8. Interior temperature: 77 °F

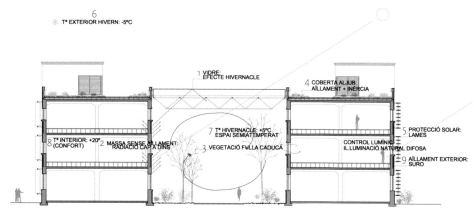

Bioclimatic diagram (winter)

1. Glass: greenhouse effect
2. Uninsulated mass
3. Deciduous vegetation
4. Green roof: inertia + insulation
5. Louvers for solar protection
6. Exterior temperature: 41 °F
7. Courtyard temperature: 41 °F
8. Interior temperature: 68 °F
9. Exterior insulation (cork)

ESQUEMA BIOCLIMÀTIC
CICLE DE L'AIGUA
e. 1/150

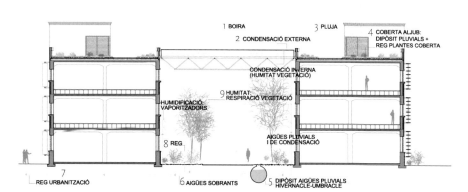

Bioclimatic diagram (water cycle)

1. Fog
2. External condensation
3. Rain
4. Rainwater tank
5. Greenhouse rainwater tank
6. Excess water
7. Development area watering system
8. Watering system
9. Internal condensation

The H-shaped buildings favor cross-ventilation
through their wings. The warmed air from the
courtyards is used to cool or warm the interior spaces.
Lider, Ecotect, Energy Plus, and Design Builder
simulation programs were used to design this.

Level 3

Level 2

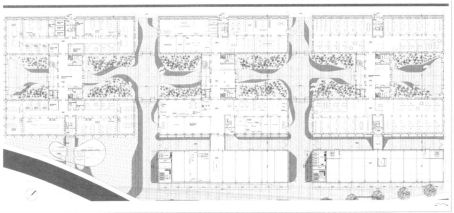

Level 1

HARMONIA 57

São Paulo, Brazil   2008

Located in a markedly artistic district on the west side of São Paulo, this is a living building that breathes, sweats, and changes. The outer walls are thick and are covered with a mantle of plants that act like a skin. The building is somewhat rough, but it exudes a certain primitive elegance. The facade is made of concrete with holes out of which plants grow. Most of the plants are epiphytes, which tend to grow on rocks in the African and Indian rainforests and which do not put roots into the soil but grow on other plant species. They are grown in a base of cement and mineral salts.

The pipes, pumps, and water treatment system are exposed, as if they were the arteries and veins of the building. From an environmental perspective, the design responds to local rainfall conditions—some 51 in/year—which is the equivalent of 61,816 gallons of good quality water mainly concentrated in the period between December and March.

The green roof gives off coolness and prevents excess humidity, regulating the temperature of the building and doing away with the need for air-conditioning. The water collected by the roof, nearly 50%, is sent to three underground storage tanks. It is then used for plant watering, plumbing, and cleaning. It is estimated that the almost eight hundred gallons a year of drinking water the building needs can be covered by rainwater.

ARCHITECT
Triptyque

CLIENT
Private

COLLABORATORS
Peter Webb (landscaping), Aparecido Donizete Dias Flausino (consultant), Guilherme Castanha (hydraulic engineering)

TOTAL SURFACE AREA
11,850 sq ft

COST
USD 406,500

PROGRAM
Artists' studio

Photography © Nelson Kon, Beto Consorte, Greg Bousquet

The facade of this home opens out as a series of
terraces on the second and third floors and with
sunshades made from timber louvers.

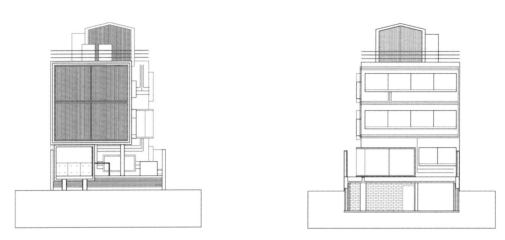

Front and rear elevations

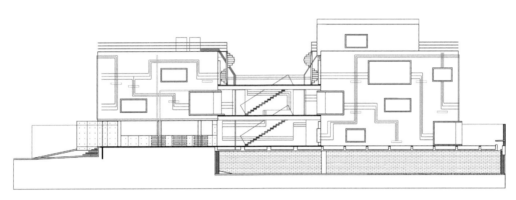

Longitudinal section

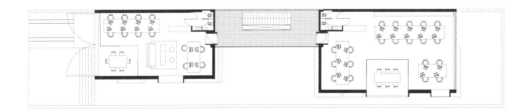

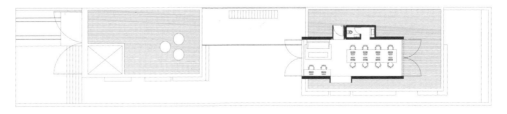

3rd floor and roof plan

Far from being hidden away, the pipes of the watering system form a striking exoskeleton that gives personality to the design. This network of pipes has a series of vertical sprinklers that supply water automatically.

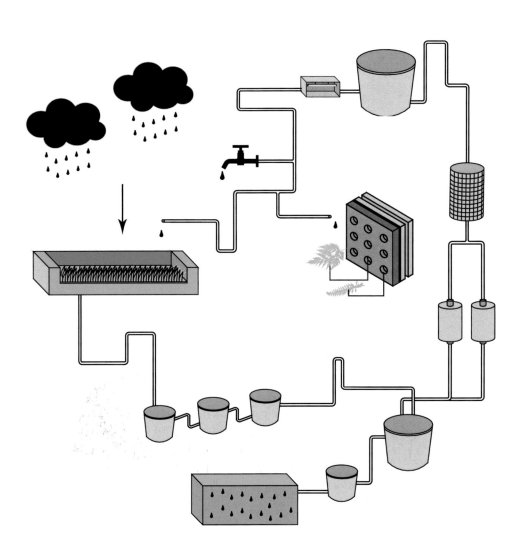

Plan of water collection and distribution

KIELDER OBSERVATORY

Kielder Water & Forest Park, United Kingdom   2008

This astronomical observatory is located in a wooded area near the England-Scotland border and Kielder Water. Kielder Water, a reservoir dating from 1980, was used until recently to supply water to support heavy industry in the Tyneside and Teesside areas, which have been in serious decline and have been disappearing in recent years. One particular feature of this area is that it has the cleanest air in England.

The program required the construction of an economical building to house two telescopes and also a room for scientific research or mixed use that could receive visits from the astronomy-loving public.

The observatory had to face south, so it was designed with an elongated shape that made the most of the hillside. The separation between the two telescope turrets resulted in an observation deck open to amateur sky gazers.

The prefabricated structure has a useful life of twenty-five years. It is transportable and, if necessary, can be moved to another location during this time. The architect designed it to be built in the locally grown Sitka spruce and Siberian larch, as they are natural materials that produce a rustic feel in a space with Victorian engineering, unlike the high-tech appearance of NASA complexes. Douglas-fir was used for the frame members and European sequoia for the struts.

The environmental aims of the facility are also seen in the decision to install a composting toilet, which avoids having to use water, given the potential freezing risk of water pipes in sub-zero winter temperatures.

The site is very windy so a 2.5-kW wind turbine was installed to use wind energy to power the building. When there is no wind blowing, ten 130-kW photovoltaic panels keep the batteries charged.

ARCHITECT
Charles Barclay Architects

CLIENT
Kielder Partnership

COLLABORATORS
Michael Hadi Associates (structural engineering), Burke Hunter Adams (quantity surveyors), Charles Barclay (astronomy consultant)

TOTAL SURFACE AREA
2,700 sq ft

COST
USD 702,000

PROGRAM
Astronomical observatory

Photography © Charles Barclay Architects, David Grandorge

The building features two telescopes (Pulsar and Meade). When both turrets are closed, the structure has the look of an austere modernist pavilion; when the turrets turn and the doors open, an expressive transformation takes place.

Site plan

Sketch

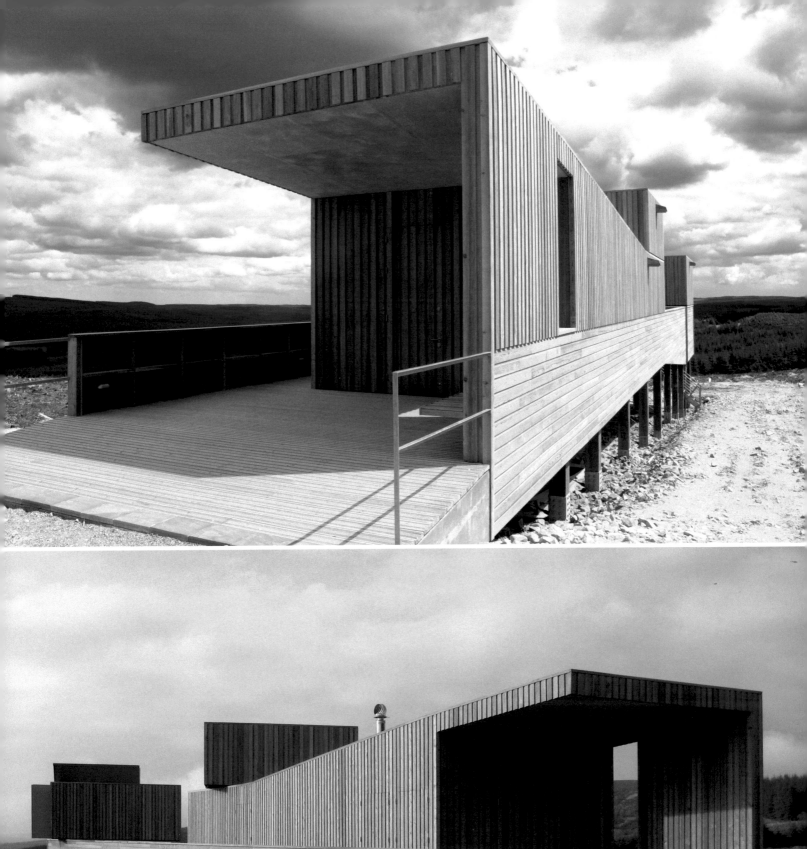

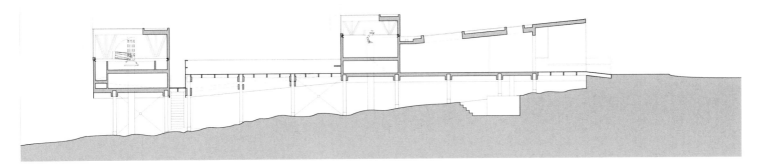

Longitudinal section

Floor plan

The revolving turrets were built as steel octagons
with eight wheels over a central track. The revolving
mechanisms are hand operated, each moving a turret
weighing more than 6 1/2 tons.

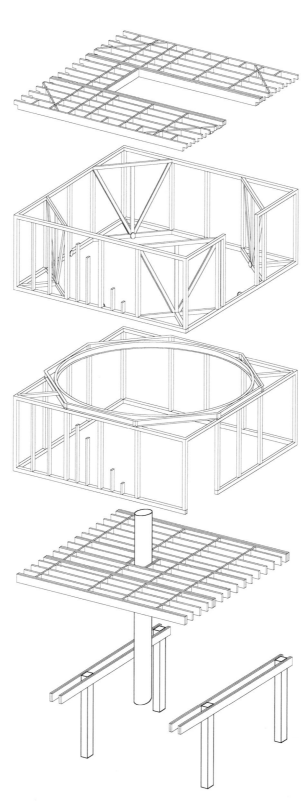

Exploded isometric view of a turret

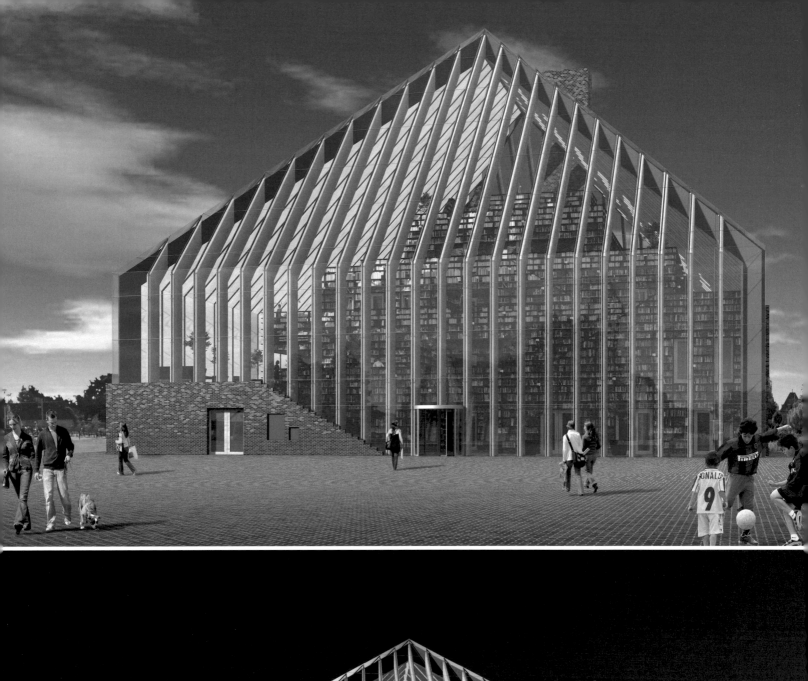

SPIJKENISSE PUBLIC LIBRARY

Spijkenisse, Netherlands   2011

The program consisted of building a public space that incorporated intelligent, low-energy environmental technology while not requiring an overly large investment.

The building has a timber frame with glass walls. The floor is fitted with radiant floor cooling featuring cold water flows to offset the heat accumulating through the entry of sunlight and body heat. This system operates by releasing cold air under the shelves. The clean cold air removes the less dense hot air by pushing it up to the ceiling. A heat exchanger allows the hot air to be used to heat the cold incoming air in winter. The cold-heat pump operates with cold-heat storage tanks in the basement. The heat stored in summer can serve to warm the space in winter, and vice versa.

The facades have automatic sun protection systems and a ventilated second skin formed by sunshades. This system filters 90% of solar radiation, preventing excess heat. The roof collects rainwater, which is used in toilets, watering plants, fire protection, and the adiabatic air-conditioning system. It is made of a heat transfer material, with a saline solution that melts or solidifies at what is close to a comfortable temperature for humans. This increases the thermal mass of the building and prevents temperature fluctuations inside. The temperature at night is reduced through the ventilation systems and solidification of the fluid.

ARCHITECT
MVRDV

CLIENT
Spijkenisse City Council

COLLABORATORS
Bouwhaven (collaborating architect), ABT (structure), Arcadis (systems installations), DGMR (acoustic and thermal insulation), Roukens + van Gils (interior design), ARUP (lighting)

SURFACE AREA
108,000 sq ft

COST
USD 10,850,000

PROGRAM
Public library

Renderings © MVRDV

The cool exterior is heated in summer by the adiabatic effect. The system sprays water into the interior air, cooling it. This cool air enters the heat exchanger and extracts heat from the incoming air. Additional cooling of incoming air in summer is provided by the cold accumulated in the underground collector.

70

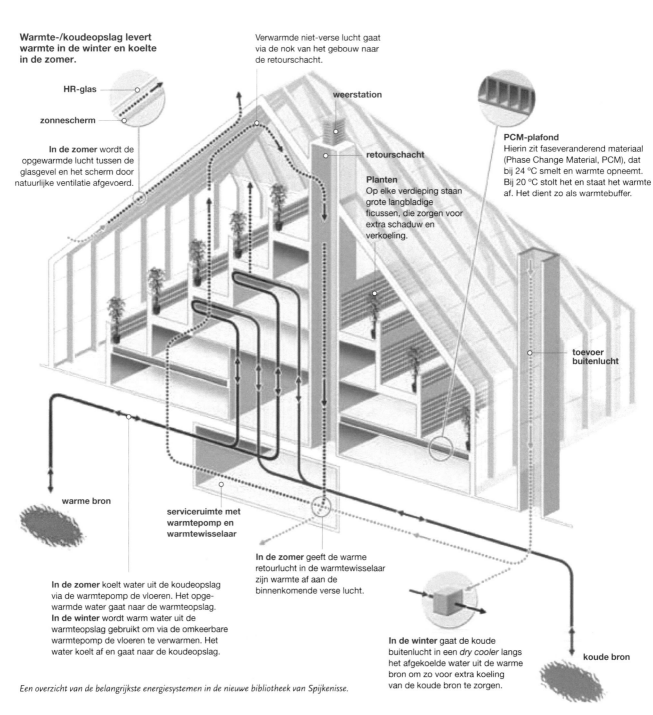

Warmte-/koudeopslag levert warmte in de winter en koelte in de zomer.

HR-glas

zonnescherm

In de zomer wordt de opgewarmde lucht tussen de glasgevel en het scherm door natuurlijke ventilatie afgevoerd.

Verwarmde niet-verse lucht gaat via de nok van het gebouw naar de retourschacht.

weerstation

retourschacht

Planten
Op elke verdieping staan grote langbladige ficussen, die zorgen voor extra schaduw en verkoeling.

PCM-plafond
Hierin zit faseveranderend materiaal (Phase Change Material, PCM), dat bij 24 °C smelt en warmte opneemt. Bij 20 °C stolt het en staat het warmte af. Het dient zo als warmtebuffer.

toevoer buitenlucht

warme bron

serviceruimte met warmtepomp en warmtewisselaar

In de zomer koelt water uit de koudeopslag via de warmtepomp de vloeren. Het opgewarmde water gaat naar de warmteopslag.
In de winter wordt warm water uit de warmteopslag gebruikt om via de omkeerbare warmtepomp de vloeren te verwarmen. Het water koelt af en gaat naar de koudeopslag.

In de zomer geeft de warme retourlucht in de warmtewisselaar zijn warmte af aan de binnenkomende verse lucht.

In de winter gaat de koude buitenlucht in een *dry cooler* langs het afgekoelde water uit de warme bron om zo voor extra koeling van de koude bron te zorgen.

koude bron

Een overzicht van de belangrijkste energiesystemen in de nieuwe bibliotheek van Spijkenisse.

Adiabatic system

ZOMER
vloer warmt op
warmte wordt in warmtebron opgeslagen
water uit koudebron wordt gebruikt voor vloerkoeling en luchtkoeling

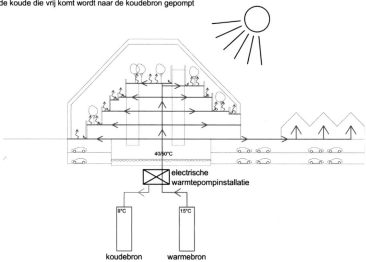

electrische
warmtepompinstallatie

9°C
15°C

koudebron   warmebron

Adiabatic system (summer)

WINTER
de temp. van de warmtebron wordt verhoogt en gebruikt voor vloerverwarming en luchtverwarming
de koude die vrij komt wordt naar de koudebron gepompt

40/50°C

electrische
warmtepompinstallatie

9°C
15°C

koudebron   warmebron

Adiabatic system (winter)

sprinklerinstallatie
regenwater wordt via de goot opgevangen
het regenwater wordt zo veel mogelijk gebruikt voor:
- toiletspoeling
- bewatering beplanting
- koeling luchtbehandeling
- waterberging sprinklerinstallatie

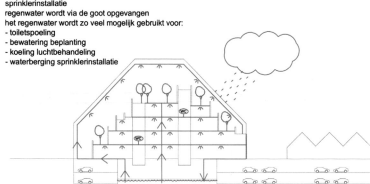

Spray system

hoogwaardige zonwerende beglazing met transparante eigenschappen

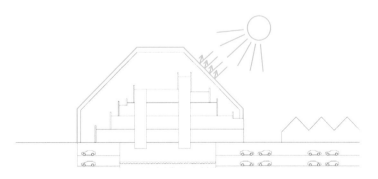

tussen glas en binnenzonwering zit een spouw
via deze spouw wordt de warme lucht weg geventileerd

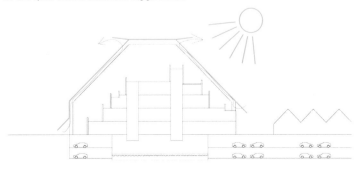

Adiabatic system

GLENEAGLES COMMUNITY CENTRE

Vancouver, British Columbia, Canada   2003

Located next to a municipal golf course, this building is laid out over three stories to minimize its carbon footprint. Entry to the main level from the street is through a porch, giving visitors access to a facility containing a community hall, cafeteria, meeting room, and administration and child day care areas.

The structural frame of the building is concrete. It has glass and concrete walls and a timber roof. The frame is a major component of the building's heating-cooling system. The concrete parts act as a powerful thermal mass, a static heat pump that absorbs, stores, and releases energy to keep the inside temperature as steady as possible.

The heating and cooling systems use radiant surfaces, both the floors and the walls, keeping the temperature comfortable. Fluid is stored by a water-to-water heat pump connected to a geothermal energy network under the parking area. Renewal of interior air is achieved through a heat-recovery ventilation system.

The bioclimatic design and arrangement of high-thermal-mass materials explains why this building only needs 40% of the energy required by a commercial building of these dimensions in the same climate region. The cantilevered roof protects against the winter rains and the strong sun in summer.

ARCHITECT
Patkau Architects

CLIENT
District of West Vancouver

COLLABORATORS
Maurice J. Ouellette Consulting, Vaughan Landscape Planning & Design, Fast & Epp Structural Engineers, Earth Tech Canada, Webster Engineering, Gage-Babcock & Associates, Susan Morris Specifications, Mc Squared System Design Group, Gallop/Varley

TOTAL SURFACE AREA
24,000 sq ft

COST
USD 4,472,000

ENERGY CONSUMPTION
13 kWh/sq ft/year

PROGRAM
Community and sports center

Photography © James Dow/Patkau Architects

The lower level is accessed from the rear of the
building, under a porch, and contains areas
adjoining the golf course, including a gymnasium,
a multipurpose room, and arts, youth, and outdoor
areas.

Site plan

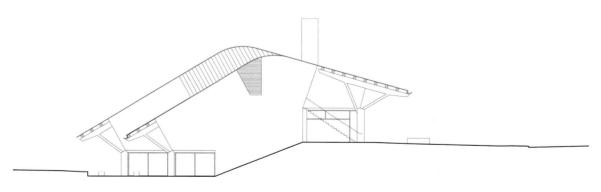

South elevation

The upper floor contains a fitness center. The gymnasium rises through the three levels, meaning that the fitness spaces and the court areas are only separated by a glass partition.

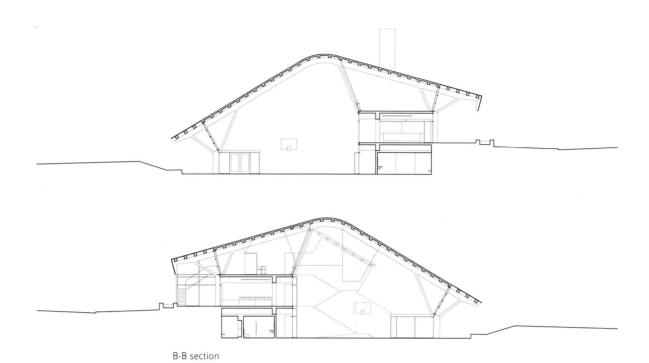

B-B section

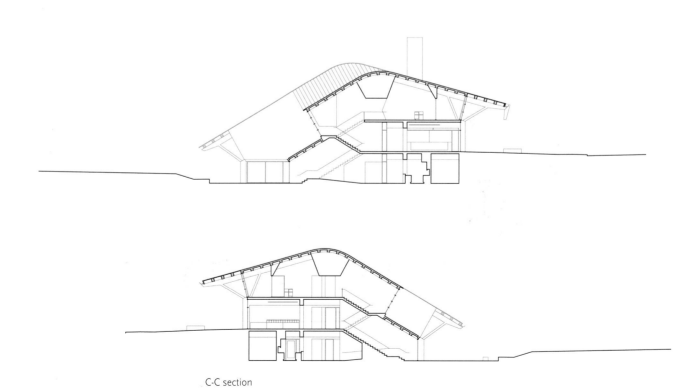

C-C section

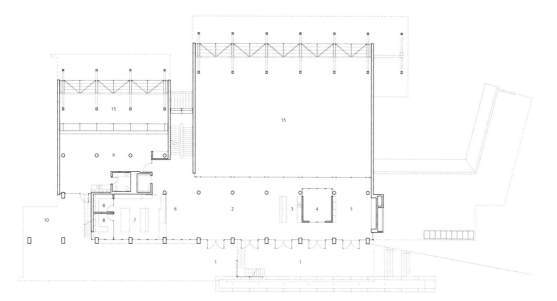

Main level

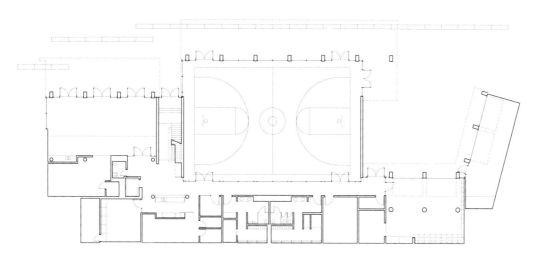

Lower level

1 Entry Porch	14 Counseling
2 "Living Room"	15 Open to Below
3 Cafe	16 Workshop
4 Meeting Room	17 Art Studio
5 Fire Place Lounge	18 Maintenance
6 Reception	19 Mechanical
7 Administration	20 Electrical
8 Office	21 Workshop Courtyard
9 Childcare	22 Kitchen
10 Children's Playground	23 Youth Lounge
11 Fitness	24 Gymnasium
12 Reception	25 Storage
13 Training Studio	26 Multipurpose

0   20 ft

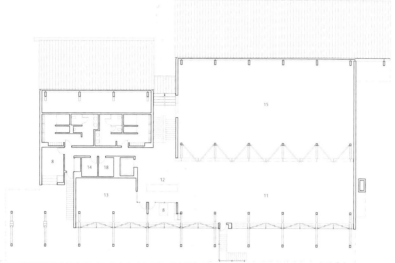

Upper level

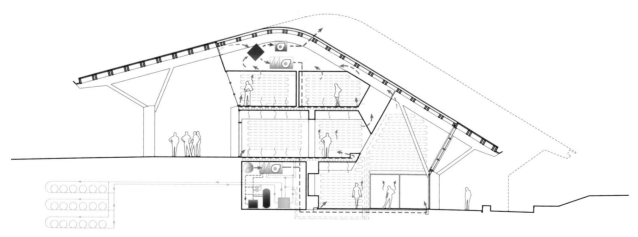

<table>
<tr><td>0   20 ft</td></tr>
</table>

1 Entry Porch	14 Counseling
2 "Living Room"	15 Open to Below
3 Cafe	16 Workshop
4 Meeting Room	17 Art Studio
5 Fire Place Lounge	18 Maintenance
6 Reception	19 Mechanical
7 Administration	20 Electrical
8 Office	21 Workshop Courtyar
9 Childcare	22 Kitchen
10 Children's Playground	23 Youth Lounge
11 Fitness	24 Gymnasium
12 Reception	25 Storage
13 Training Studio	26 Multipurpose

mechanical services section

Radiant heating and heat-recovery ventilation system

SIEEB – SINO-ITALIAN ECOLOGICAL AND ENERGY-EFFICIENT BUILDING

Beijing, China   2006

The SIEEB building is a platform for the bilateral cooperation between Italy and China in the fields of energy and environmental preservation efforts. It is also a showcase building for reducing CO_2 emissions in the construction sector in China.

The building features spaces for research and teaching, in addition to offices and a two hundred-seat auditorium. The design incorporates passive and active strategies in its form and skin to control the external environment and improve interior air quality.

The north-facing facade is closed and highly insulated, given that the cold winter winds come from this direction. The facade becomes more transparent toward the south. On the east and west sides, sunlight and radiation are controlled through the double glass skin. To the south, can-tilevered structures provide shade for the terraces.

The building features a bioclimatic design. It combines the use of glass for natural lighting with renewable energies and rainwater collection by means of roof cisterns.

The offices and laboratories located on the upper floors have terraced gardens that also use cisterns. Together with overhanging structures, where the photovoltaic panels are located, they act as sunshades for the floor directly below. These sustainability efforts enable the SIEEB to emit around 550 short tons of CO_2 per year, compared to the average of 3,860 tons emitted by a conventional building, with a 50% saving on air-conditioning usage and costs.

ARCHITECT
Mario Cucinella Architects

CLIENT
The Italian Ministry for the Environment and Territory and the Chinese Ministry of Science and Technology

COLLABORATORS
Favero & Milan Ingegneria, China Architecture Design & Research Group

TOTAL SURFACE AREA
215,300 sq ft

COST
USD 27,758,000

ENERGY CONSUMPTION
1.5 kWh/sq ft/year (electricity), 99 cu ft/sq ft/year (gas)

PROGRAM
University designed as a joint venture between Italy and China

Photography © Daniele Domenicali

The south facade is open and permeable. The interior
skin makes use of different ventilated facade systems.

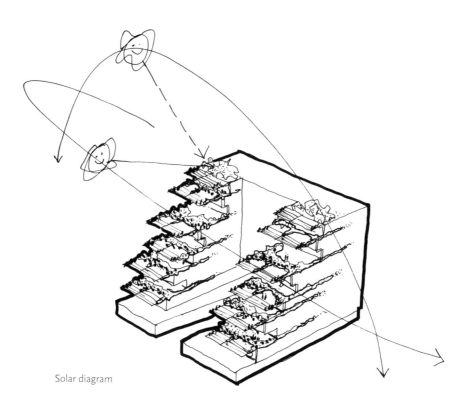

Solar diagram

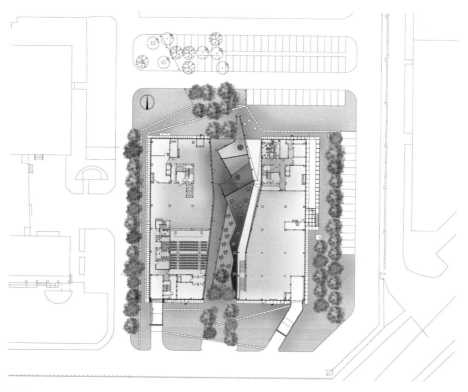

Site Plan

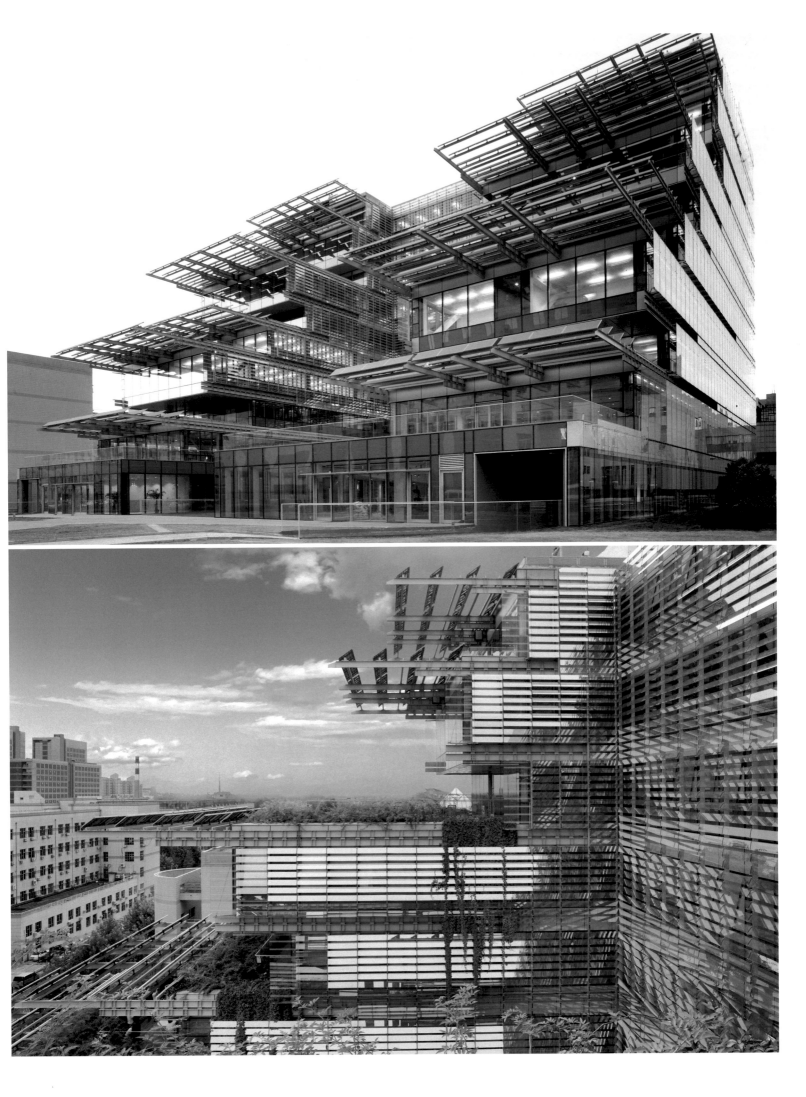

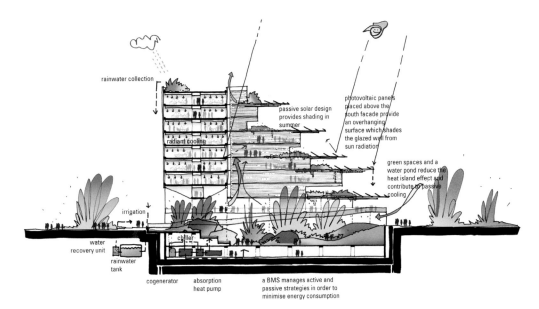

rainwater collection

passive solar design
provides shading in
summer

photovoltaic panels
placed above the
south facade provide
an overhanging
surface which shades
the glazed wall from
sun radiation

radiant cooling

green spaces and a
water pond reduce the
heat island effect and
contribute to passive
cooling

irrigation

water
recovery unit

chiller

rainwater
tank

cogenerator   absorption
heat pump

a BMS manages active and
passive strategies in order to
minimise energy consumption

Section with environmental features (summer)

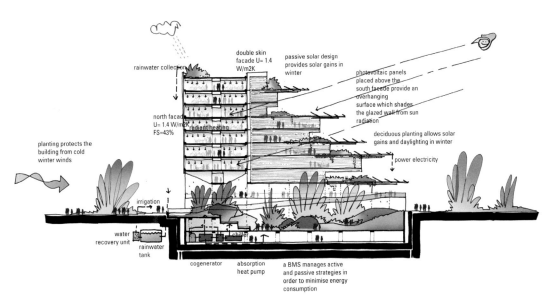

double skin
facade U= 1.4
W/m2K

passive solar design
provides solar gains in
winter

rainwater collection

photovoltaic panels
placed above the
south facade provide
an overhanging
surface which shades
the glazed wall from sun
radiation

north facade
U= 1.4 W/m2K
FS=43%

radiant heating

deciduous planting allows solar
gains and daylighting in winter

planting protects the
building from cold
winter winds

power electricity

irrigation

water
recovery unit

chiller

rainwater
tank

cogenerator   absorption
heat pump

a BMS manages active
and passive strategies in
order to minimise energy
consumption

Section with environmental features (winter)

The north facade is thicker than the south facade, with heavier insulation and opacity to protect the building from cold winter winds. The east and west have a double skin comprising a curtain wall and a simple glass skin.

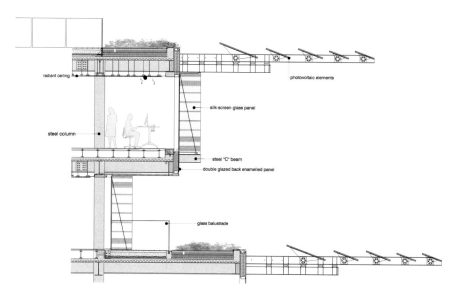

radiant ceiling

photovoltaic elements

silk-screen glass panel

steel column

steel "C" beam

double glazed back enamelled panel

glass balustrade

South facade section in detail

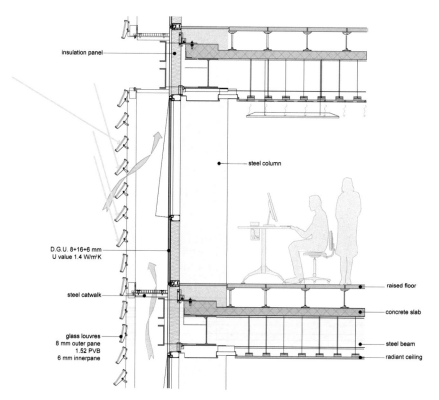

insulation panel

steel column

D.G.U. 8+16+6 mm
U value 1.4 W/m²K

steel catwalk

raised floor

concrete slab

glass louvres
8 mm outer pane
1.52 PVB
6 mm innerpane

steel beam

radiant ceiling

Section east facade

AZ-VUB UNIVERSITY HOSPITAL OF BRUSSELS

Brussels, Belgium   2007

The construction of this annex was part of the master plan for remodeling the university hospital in Brussels. The master plan involved reorganizing doctors' offices and redesigning the parking lot.

The program limited the building's height to nine stories. In response to this limitation, two basement levels were initially considered, but this underground solution was finally ruled out for technical reasons (problems with waste management and the wastewater pump) and occupational reasons (it was considered that working without sunlight is not advisable).

The final designed building combines the advantages of an underground building with those of a building standing at street level. The higher floors are where offices are located, while the lower floors, which are larger and multifunctional, hold laboratories. A series of peripheral passageways, with a two-story height, wrap around the laboratory and technical office areas. It is planned that there will be future extension of the building over the parking lot.

The building has a green facade, and its walkways serve as thermal chambers. The south and north facades hold metal screens to filter light and prevent overheating. Its skin is made from a hydrophilic layer with volcanic soil where ivy and other plant species can grow, helping the building to integrate with its green surroundings.

ARCHITECT
Samyn and Partners Architects & Engineers

CLIENT
University Hospital of Brussels

COLLABORATORS
Jan Tewercoren, Matthieu Veldekens, Steven Godemont, François Smal, Anne Remue

TOTAL SURFACE AREA
55,500 sq ft

COST
USD 13,000,000

PROGRAM
Building for university hospital laboratories, administration offices, and doctors' offices

Photography © Marie-Françoise Plissart

An extension to the hospital complex was achieved in
a way that incorporated bioclimatic architecture and
met the challenges of the site, while respecting the
views over Brussels from the existing building.

Side elevation

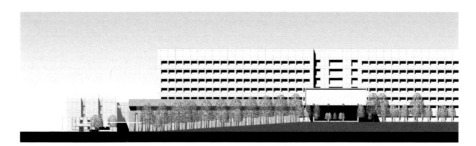

Longitudinal elevation

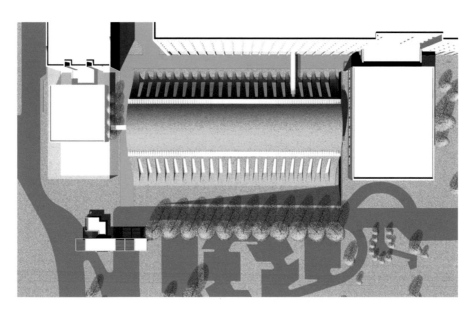

Ground plan

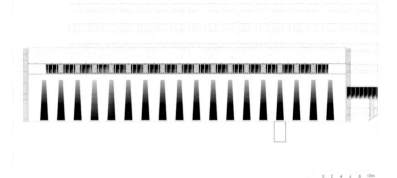

Longitudinal elevation

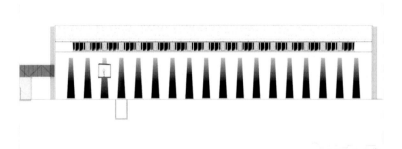

West elevation

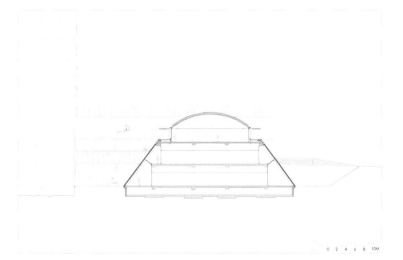

East elevation

The peripheral ring surrounding the laboratories and offices filters light through vertical openings in its facade. Like the green facade, this area between the interior and exterior acts as a thermal chamber.

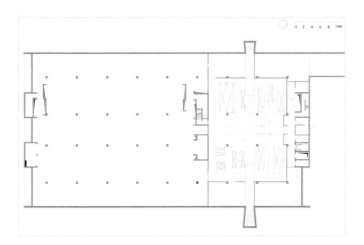

Level −2 (control room)

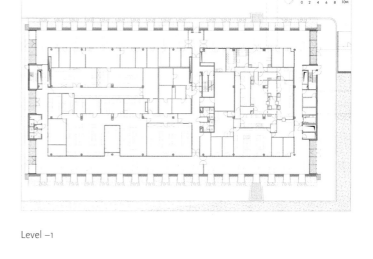

Level −1

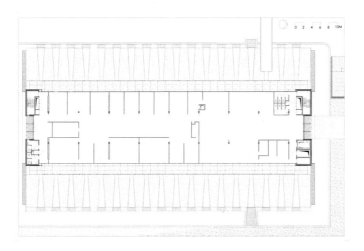

Level 2

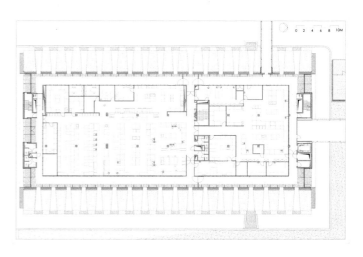

Level 1

THE MAIN STADIUM
FOR THE WORLD GAMES 2009

Kaohsiung, Taiwan   2009

Host city for the 2009 World Games, Kaohsiung is the second-most populous city in Taiwan. The World Games is an event reserved for sports not included in the Olympic Games program. It is held every four years, one year after the Olympic Games are held.

Kaohsiung stadium was the main venue of the games held in July 2009. It normally seats forty thousand spectators, but has the possibility to increase its capacity to fifty-five thousand with temporary bleachers. It is the first stadium in Taiwan to hold the Class-1 standard of the International Association of Athletics Federations (IAAF) and Federation Internationale de Football Association (FIFA) standard.

The key design concepts used in its construction were: open stadium, urban park, and spiral continuum. The stadium had to be accessible on days when no events were being held, which explains the large front esplanade and the opening on the south facade. The spiral continuum refers to the 237,000 sq ft roof with photovoltaic panels assembled from laminated safety glass. This dynamic and curved roof is made up of three layers comprising: a) 159 trusses of different sizes as their main structural element; b) thirty-two oscillating rings that connect all of the trusses and give them the feel of a spiral continuum (these rings also have a structural function against possible seismic movements and strong winds); c) photovoltaic panels with variable widths between 1 and 1.5 in. The locks connecting them to the oscillating rings allow the angle and position of each panel to be adjusted.

ARCHITECT
Ito · Takenaka · RLA Kaohsiung Main Stadium for 2009 World Games Design Team

CLIENT
National Council on Physical Fitness and Sports (NCPFS), Executive Yuan / Bureau of Public Works City of Kaohsiung

COLLABORATORS
Fu Tsu Construction Co. Ltd., Takenaka Corporation + Hsin-Yeh Engineering Consultants Inc. (structural engineering), Takenaka Corporation + Teddy & Associates (mechanical engineering), Engineering Consultants, Ltd. + C. C. LEE & Associates Hvacr Consulting Engineers (mechanical engineering), Lancaster Co., Ltd. (lighting), Takenaka Corporation + Laboratory for Environment & Form (landscaping), Takenaka Corporation + Ricky Liu & Associates Architects + Planners (interior design), Lead Dao Technology and Engineering Ltd. (3-D models)

TOTAL SURFACE AREA
1,063,000 sq ft

CERTIFICATION
Gold Award for Green Building (Taiwan)

PROGRAM
Main stadium for the 2009 World Games

Photography © Fu Tsu Construction Co., Ltd.

One of the requirements of the program was that
the stadium be open. Unlike most stadiums, which
are closed for their entire perimeter, the one in
Kaohsiung is open on the south side to offer visitors
views of the city.

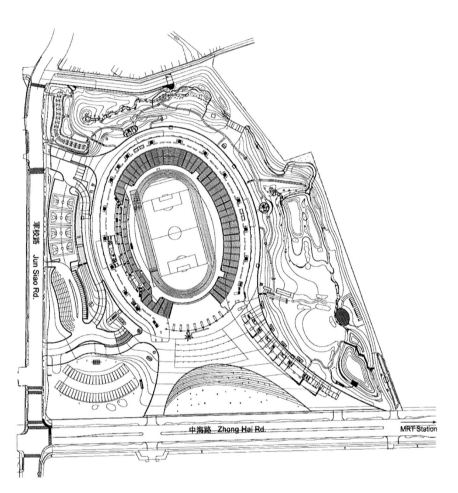

Site plan

Approximately 140,000 sq ft of the roof is covered
with 8,800 photovoltaic panels, with a capacity of
1,000 kWh, and producing 1,100,000 kW per year. This
represents a reduction of 727 short tons of CO_2.

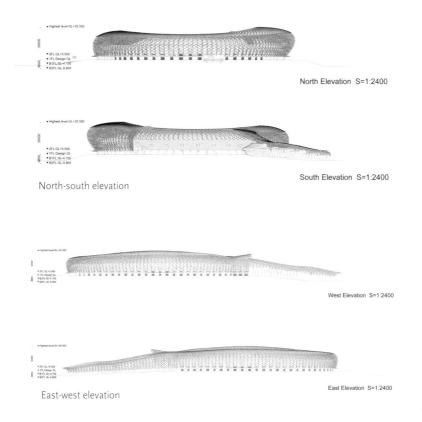

North Elevation S=1:2400

South Elevation S=1:2400

North-south elevation

West Elevation S=1:2400

East Elevation S=1:2400

East-west elevation

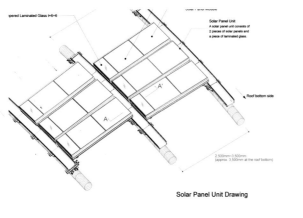

Solar Panel Unit Drawing

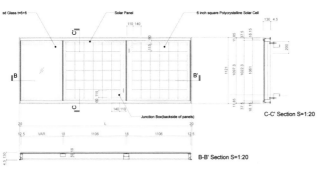

Solar Panel Unit Detailed Drawing S=1:20

Detail of photovoltaic panel

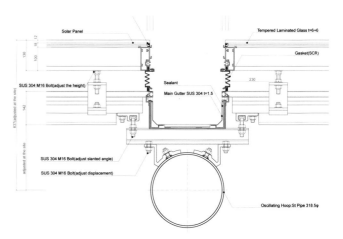

Main Gutter Part Detailed Drawing(A-A' Cross Section) S=1:5

ALILA VILLAS ULUWATU

Uluwatu, Indonesia, 2009

This resort is located in a savanna-like landscape on the cliffs of the Bukit Peninsula, in the south of the island of Bali. It comprises fifty resort villas and thirty-five residential villas. Each resort villa has a pool and a hut facing the sea.

The villas form terraces on the hills and consist of pavilions joined by bridges passing over water features in the gardens. The design seeks integration with the existing landscape at all times, and reproduces the limestone terraces that are features of the rural landscape in the area.

The design is a blend of vernacular architecture and contemporary design, so that the traditional architecture of the Balinese pavilion delights as much as the contemporary arrangement of space and form. It was built and is operated according to sustainable principles. The open-plan design of the resort's villas makes them appear as if they are merged into its gardens, with the outer walls of the garden used as the outer walls of the villas. As a result, actions like sleeping, eating, resting, and showering feel as if they are taking place outside.

Among the environmental features of the complex are its integration with its surrounding area; rainwater collection system; pool water recycling; gray water recycling in toilets and for plant watering; aquifer renewal by means of sumps and water percolating down from the gardens; solar protection measures to provide natural cooling; plants adapted to dry conditions in gardens; locally sourced materials and recycled rubble; wood and bamboo in furniture without toxic preservatives; nontoxic termite treatment; and, finally, job creation and involvement of the local community in complementary activities outside the hotel, a community sustainabilitiy initiative.

ARCHITECT
WOHA Designs Pte Ltd

CLIENT
Bukit Uluwatu Alila

COLLABORATORS
Makesthi Enggal Engineering (mechanical and electrical engineering), Worley Parsons Ltd, Atelier Enam Struktur (civil and structural engineering), Sustainable Built Environments (environmental consultants), Lighting Planners Associates (lighting consultants), Kosprima Sarana Kuantitama (quantity surveyor), Cicada Pte Ltd (landscaping)

TOTAL SURFACE AREA
286,000 sq ft (excludes gardens, walkways, swimming pools, and communal areas)

COST
USD 71,275,000

ENERGY CONSUMPTION
14.3 kWh/sq ft/year

CERTIFICATION
Green Globe 21

PROGRAM
Hotel and residential resort development

Photography © Patrick Bingham-Hall

The resort was designed to comply with EC3 Global's
Green Globe 21 standard requirements for certification.
This is a voluntary certification for sustainable
management in the world of tourism. In this case,
the "greening process" was influential in the design,
construction, and management stages.

Elevation

LEGEND

1 ENTRY ROAD
2 HOTEL PUBLIC AREAS
3 LIMESTONE CLIFF
4 CLIFF SIDE VILLAS
5 HOTEL VILLAS
6 HILLSIDE VILLAS

ALILA VILLAS, ULUWATU
MASTER PLAN & SECTION

0   50   100   200 M

1 : 5000 A4

WOHA DESIGNS PTE LTD / WOHA ARCHITECTS PTE LTD
2008
© WOHA Pte Ltd DEC 2003. All rights reserved.

Site plan

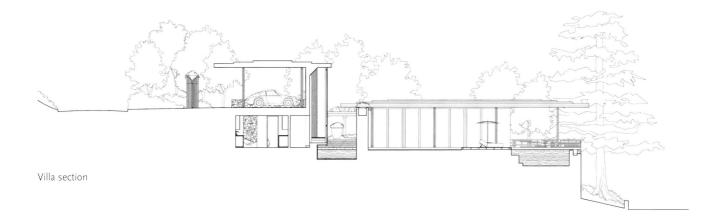

Villa section

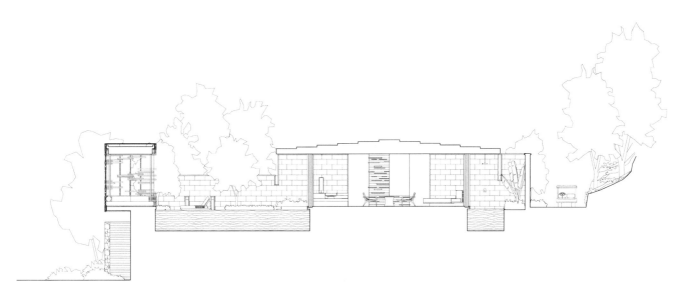

Resort villa section

Materials used were sourced locally or from neighboring Java, including coconut fibers and bamboo. Craftsmen on the islands of Java and Bali were commissioned for the design and creation of interior furnishings.

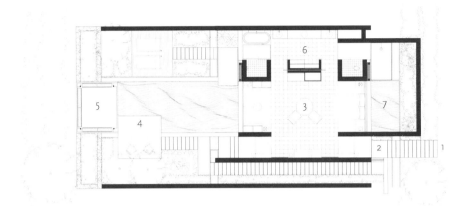

1. Walkway
2. Entrance
3. Living area
4. Pool and terrace
5. Hut
6. Bath
7. Patio and outside shower

Resort villa floor plan

GARDUCHO BIOLOGICAL STATION

Mourão, Portugal   2009

This biology station is located close to the Guadiana River in an area protected by the European Union's Natura 2000 network. The area is classified as a Special Protection Area (SPA) for birds and a Site of Community Importance (SCI).

A reorganization project for this space began in 2005 with the aim of turning the structure into a national benchmark facility for tasks of conservation, research, environmental education, and promotion of the natural heritage of the region. The reorganization took on a functional project that remodeled the three existing buildings into a larger workspace with minimum impact on the site.

Given its location in a protected area, the building is cantilevered over a structure anchored in the ground, creating a series of courtyards and walkways between the functional areas. This semi-elevated position and the raised walkways provide spectacular views of the surrounding landscape. The complex is centered on a large courtyard, around which the different buildings, covered outdoor spaces, and walkways are laid out.

Recycled wood railroad ties were used as handrails on balconies and terraces, while recycled cork was used for insulation.

Geographically located in a remote area, the building had to be 100% self-sufficient in water and energy. Photovoltaic panels were placed on the roof and a rainwater storage cistern was also installed.

ARCHITECT
João Maria Ventura Trindade/Ventura Trindade Arquitectos

CLIENT
Iberian Avifauna Study Centre

COLLABORATORS
Paulo Cardoso, Pedro Romano/PRPC (engineers), Hugo Veríssimo, Carlos Certal (structural engineers)

TOTAL SURFACE AREA
5,300 sq ft

COST
USD 914,000

ENERGY CONSUMPTION
2.2 kWh/sq ft/year

PROGRAM
Facility for environmental conservation, research, and education

Photography © André Carvalho, José Manuel Silva

The design of the building was developed to meet its different uses. It is a place for researching its surrounding area of great natural heritage, and it is also open to the public for education and promotion purposes.

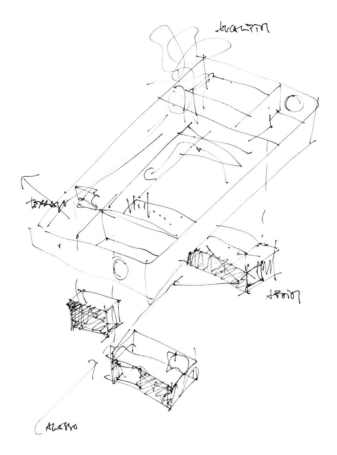

Rendering

Site plan

surgem as paisagens.

POENTE   NORTE   NASCENTE   SUL

Elevations

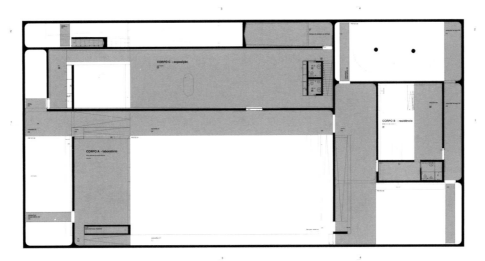

Upper level

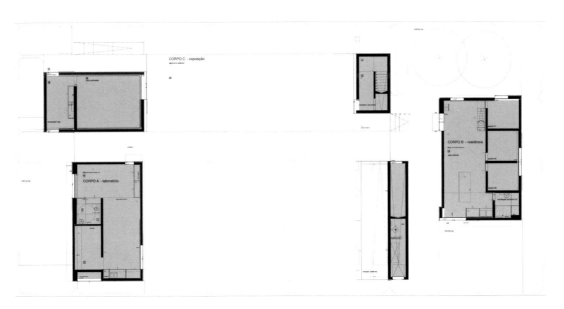

Lower level

This biology station encourages visitors to learn about the use of alternative energies, waste treatment, and rainwater harvesting.

1. Rainwater collector (area 1)
2. Rainwater collector (area 2)
3. Storage (area 1)
4. Storage (area 2)
5. Green roof
6. Cistern
7. Water tank
8. Treated water inlet
9. To wetlands

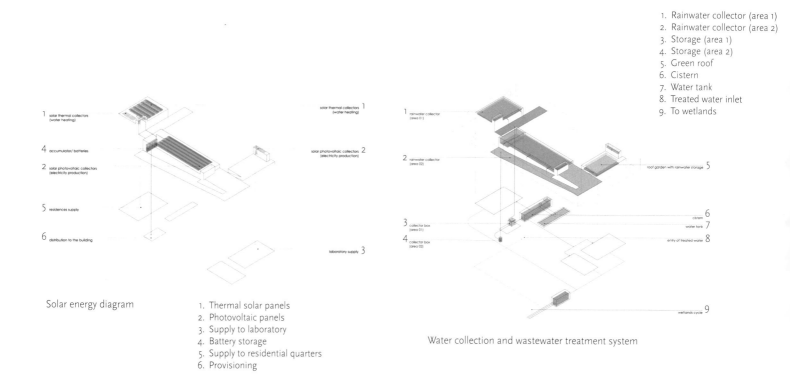

Solar energy diagram

1. Thermal solar panels
2. Photovoltaic panels
3. Supply to laboratory
4. Battery storage
5. Supply to residential quarters
6. Provisioning

Water collection and wastewater treatment system

CORPORATE

HOLCIM OFFICES

San Rafael – Alajuela, Costa Rica   2004

Bruno Stagno describes his architecture as "architecture for a latitude."

Holcim S. A. turned a desert-like rocky hilltop into an industrial area, a friendly and green place. The project combined landscaping and architecture in a complex featuring courtyards and gardens.

Holcim, a manufacturer of cement and diverse building materials, commissioned a building that would reflect the possibilities offered by its products, without turning it into a showcase building. The design features the sophisticated use of concrete, an essentially rustic material, combined with ultralight fabrics that tone down the tectonic feel of the cement-based materials, together with tensile structures that provide shade and lower the thermal load of the building, which has no mechanical air-conditioning other than in the auditorium.

A simulation was made of the behavior of the north and south wings during the design stage. This simulation made use of the Comfort thermal model with climate data obtained from the nearest weather station. This simulation helped to achieve a lessening of the effects of sunlight on roofs and, consequently, on interior temperature.

Keeping to the principle of more design than technology, the architect achieved a complex that complies with ISO comfort standards and has a gross electricity expense of USD 0.84/ sq ft.

The use of resistant and low-maintenance materials was one of the program requirements. Fiber-cement panels were used as siding. The materials were left untreated to allow for natural aging.

ARCHITECT
Bruno Stagno

CLIENT
Holcim Costa Rica S. A.

COLLABORATORS
Juan Carlos Sotela (structural engineering), FTL Design Engineering Studio (structural engineering), Juan Luis Flores (mechanical engineering), RAE Ingenieros (construction), Jimena Ugarte (landscaping)

TOTAL SURFACE AREA
42,000 sq ft

COST:
USD 2,600,000

ENERGY CONSUMPTION
9 kWh/sq ft/year

PROGRAM
Office building

Photography © Jimena Ugarte

The building, consisting of four wings, is located on the outskirts of San Antonio de Belén and can take full advantage of breezes. The climate is characterized by its steady temperatures. Rainwater, abundant depending on the season, is collected for use in watering and air-conditioning.

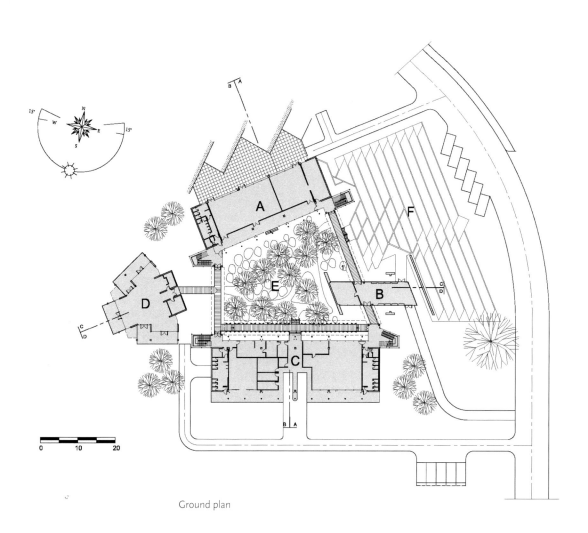

Ground plan

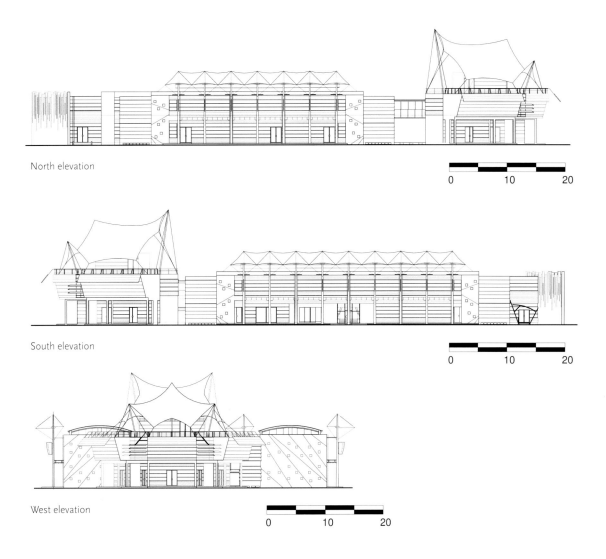

North elevation

0 10 20

South elevation

0 10 20

West elevation

0 10 20

Shade is a necessity for comfort in tropical climes.
The roof is designed to act as a sunshade, with
support from its eaves to produce shade and create a
microclimate suited to the building.

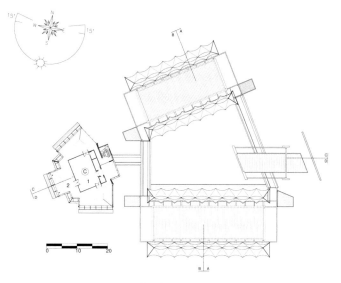

Level 3

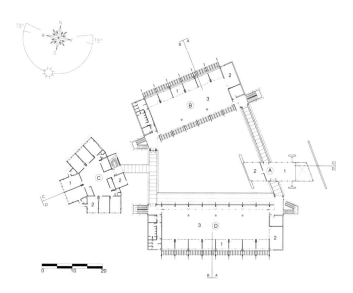

Level 2

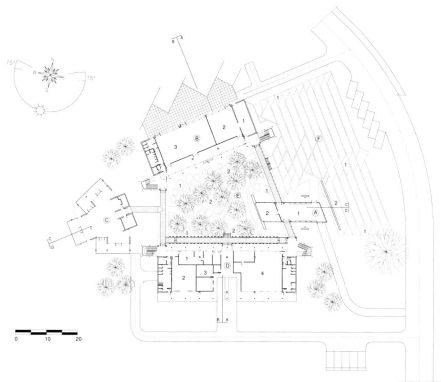

Level 1

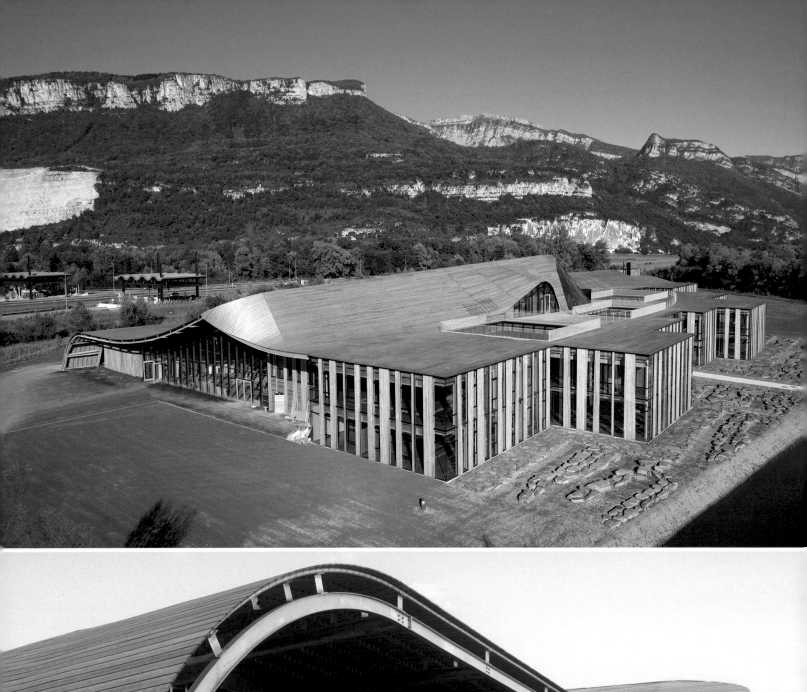

ROSSIGNOL WORLD HEADQUARTERS

La Buisse – Saint-Jean-de-Moirans, France   2009

The design of the Rossignol world headquarters was inspired by the fluid nature of skiing movements—drawing from the sentimental attachment of the brand to the world of skiing and mountain sports—and by the local landscape, which blends seamlessly with its timber roof, which mimics the surrounding mountains. This spectacular element covers three well-differentiated areas: the production and technology space, the foyer and reception area, and its offices.

The interior of the building operates like a beehive, offering permeability between the different areas of activity and online work. The project's originality lies in the way it combines varying departments and operations within the one building, such as the ski production unit, which also functions as the technological showroom, the R&D and design departments, located at the heart of the building, and two retail showrooms for presenting Rossignol and Quiksilver products.

The enhancement of social spaces is achieved in communal areas such as the restaurant, bathed in light streaming through two large glass facades affording panoramic views of the Vercors plateau.

Priority was given to making the building energy efficient and installing good insulation. The design of the structure gives it the lowest possible carbon footprint. It is protected from the summer sun by an untreated timber roof. Rainwater is collected and water from production processes is treated for reuse.

ARCHITECT
Hérault Arnod Architectes

CLIENT
Skis Rossignol SAS

COLLABORATORS
Batiserf (structure), Nicolas (fluids), Forgue (budget), Cap Paysages (landscaping)

TOTAL SURFACE AREA
125,000 sq ft

COST
USD 27,400,000

ENERGY CONSUMPTION
1.3 kWh/sq ft/year

PROGRAM
Rossignol headquarters and R&D development center

Photography © André Morin, Gilles Cabella

The irregular roofline and facades of the offices are an
allusion to the idea of constant growth.

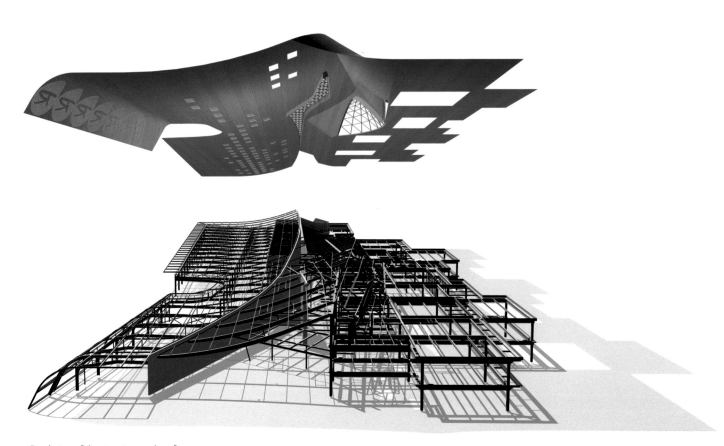

Rendering of the structure and roof

The building complies with the THPE RT2005 French thermal building regulation for thermal insulation and heating systems. To meet this, energy efficiency must be at least 15% higher than that of conventional buildings, a figure that is to rise to 40% by 2020.

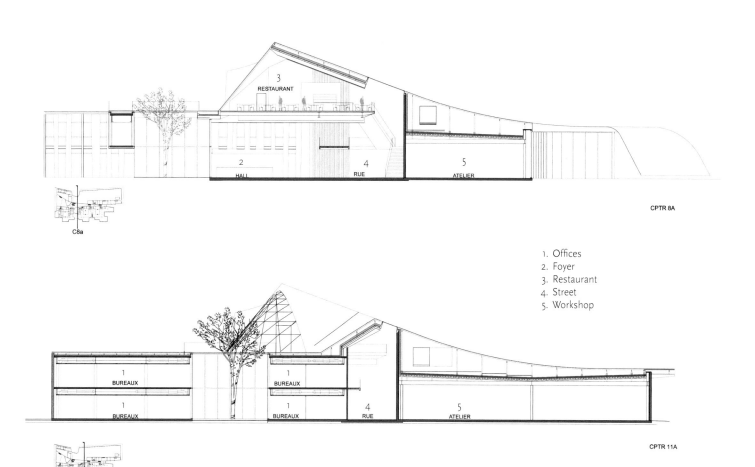

3
RESTAURANT

2
HALL

4
RUE

5
ATELIER

C8a

CPTR 8A

1. Offices
2. Foyer
3. Restaurant
4. Street
5. Workshop

1
BUREAUX

1
BUREAUX

1
BUREAUX

1
BUREAUX

1
BUREAUX

4
RUE

5
ATELIER

C11a

CPTR 11A

Longitudinal sections

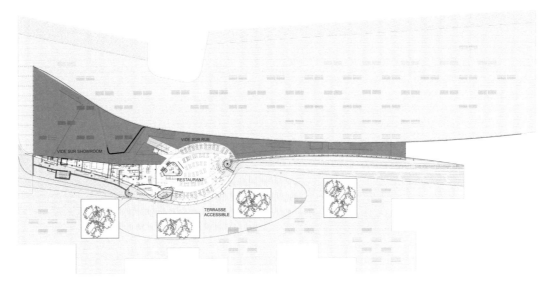

Level 3

The heat from workshop machinery is cooled and
repurposed by the air-conditioning system as an
energy-saving measure.

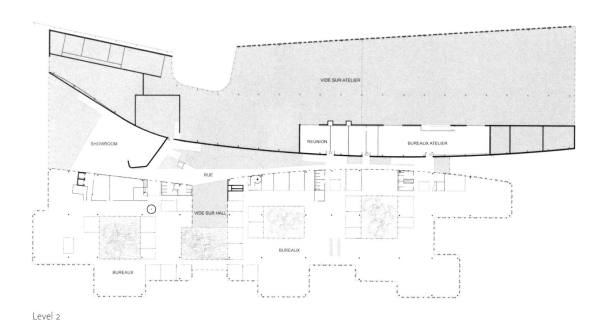

Level 2

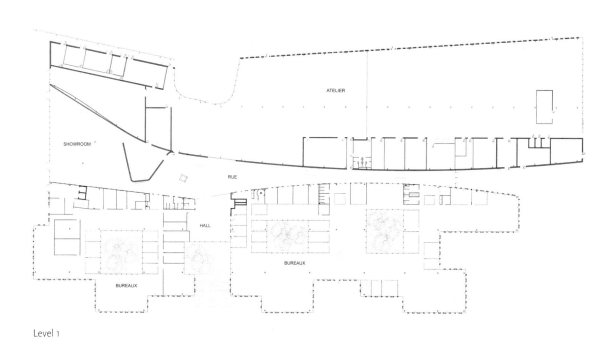

Level 1

NUEVAS BODEGAS PROTOS

Peñafiel, Spain   2008

The new Protos building combines the company's wine-making facilities, social areas, and offices in one building. The design responds to the spatial and atmospheric conditions required for the production of wine, while representing the brand and blending with the Peñafiel landscape.

The plinth of the building is anchored to the ground, evening the sloping terrain and creating a support for the light vaults that rest over it. The roof is made up of a series of parabolic arch structures in laminated timber, reinterpreting the winery building as a ship.

If every town has its own particular characteristics in its setting, whether visual or related to the landscape, Peñafiel can be said to be defined by the red-brown of its traditional roof tiles. The final colors of the roof of the new winery respond to this.

Most of the site's wine-making and aging facilities are buried below ground. They are encased in reinforced concrete, with a design that enhances heat transfer with the ground. This reduces the impact of sunlight and extreme climate conditions during the day and night and seasonal cycles.

The tile roof absorbs direct solar radiation, diffusing the heat by means of ventilation in the internal cavities of the tiles and the air chamber. In this way, heat loss is minimized, and it is accumulated by radiation in the structure of the building.

Energy savings in air-conditioning are also achieved by means of an energy management system and the use of groundwater as an integral part of cooling systems.

ARCHITECT
Alonso, Balaguer y Arquitectos Asociados and RSHP – Rogers, Stirk, Harbour + Partners

CLIENT
Protos Bodega Ribera de Duero de Peñafiel, S.L.

COLLABORATORS
CEM (project management), Tecnics G3 (budgetary control), Agroindus (installation and structural engineering, and budgetary control), Jose María Garrido (quantity surveyor), BOMA (structural engineering), BDSP Partnership (budgetary control), Grupo JG (installation engineering), Arup (structural engineering), Biosca & Botey (lighting consultants), FCC (builders), Prefabricados Pujol (prefabricated framework), Holtza (laminated timber frame), Folcra (curtain walls)

TOTAL SURFACE AREA
234,000 sq ft

COST
USD 48,756,000

ENERGY CONSUMPTION
6 kWh/sq ft/year

PROGRAM
Winery

Photography © Josep Mffi Molinos

The roof of the light vaults protects the building from
direct solar radiation on its glazed facade, which is
set back 30 ft under an overhang on the south face
and 60 ft on the east. A brise-soleil system protects
the west facade.

Rendering

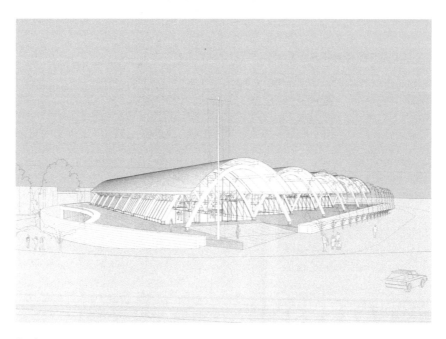

Rendering

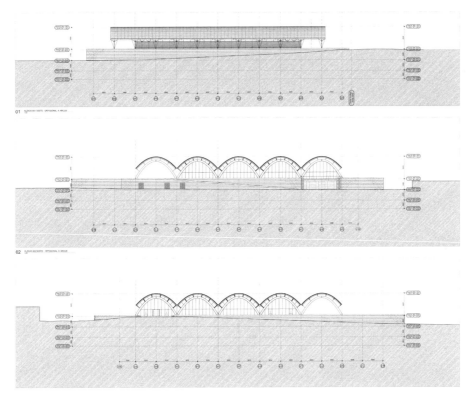

Elevations

Rendering

The plinth is buried to take advantage of thermal ground mass. It houses the wine-making and aging areas. The design is a contemporary take on traditional winery construction.

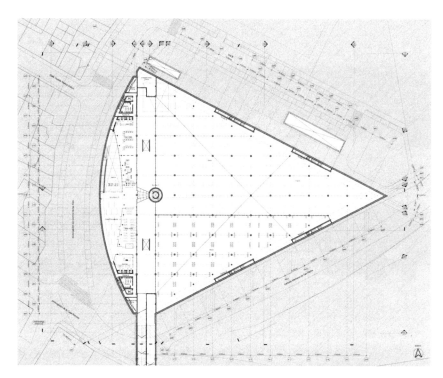

Upper level floor plan

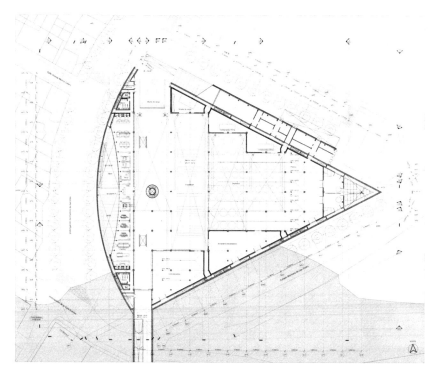

Wine-making area floor plan

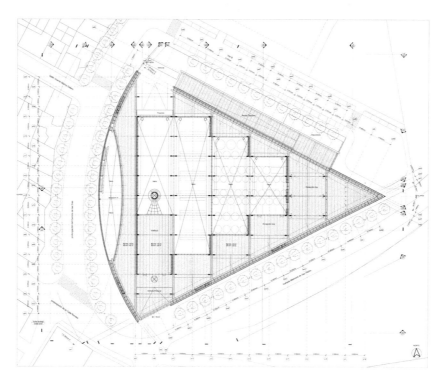

Entrance area floor plan

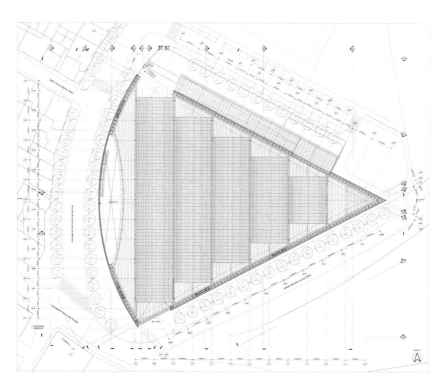

Roof plan

BAUSPARKASSE WÜSTENROT

Salzburg, Austria   2005

To celebrate its eightieth anniversary, Bausparkasse Wüstenrot, a bank that finances property development projects, commissioned the remodeling of the 1960s building housing its Salzburg office. The new building was to be unique and iconic, and to become a recognized feature of the Salzburg-Süd district where it stands.

The building is laid out around a lobby-reception area, leading to an "info-lounge" and banking consultants' private offices.

The entire remodeling was focused on ecology and energy. The complex is clad in a transparent skin formed by perforated steel plates and a modular system of sunshades that can be controlled from individual offices.

The effect of light on the double metallic skin creates a natural light show during the day and generates different color patterns of the building. The concrete facade behind the skin was insulated with mineral wool and lined with large serigraphic glass panels to protect it from moisture. The remodeling also used mineral wool to replace its polystyrol insulation.

The facade is printed with plant motifs, reflecting the image of one of the oak trees standing in front of the building. The facades facing the atrium feature motifs also inspired by oak leaves.

The old aluminum windows were changed to wood-framed, insulated glass windows. The remodeling has lead to energy saving of approximately 60%.

ARCHITECT
Trauner.Strobl.Bach Architekten

CLIENT
Bausparkasse Wüstenrot AG

COLLABORATORS
Marius & Partner Ingenieure, RFG Engineering GmbH (engineering), Architekt Six Energieoptimierung (energy consultants), Michael Herbst and Ökobau Schorn (engineering)

TOTAL SURFACE AREA
172,450 sq ft

ENERGY CONSUMPTION
4 kWh/sq ft/year

PROGRAM
Remodeling of a bank building

Photography © Josephine Unterhauser

The new Bausparkasse Wüstenrot office building
stands sculpture-like with its double-skinned facade,
a perforated metal structure twisted into different
planes and producing multicolored effects when the
sun shines on it.

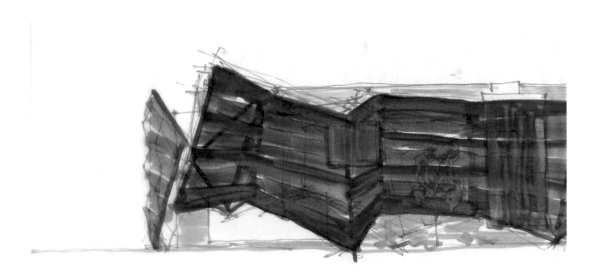

Sketch

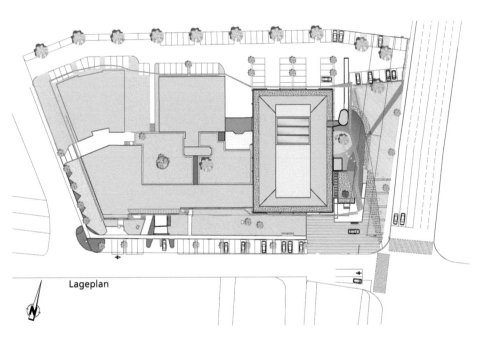

Lageplan

Site plan

North elevation

West elevation

South elevation

The lobby is housed in a glass volume that opens under the vertex where the double metallic skin converges. The interior walls are adorned with serigraph plant motifs.

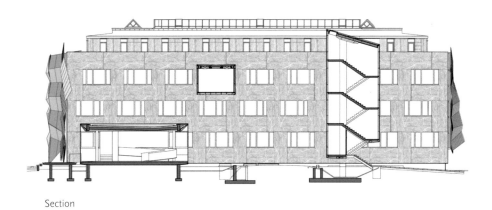

Section

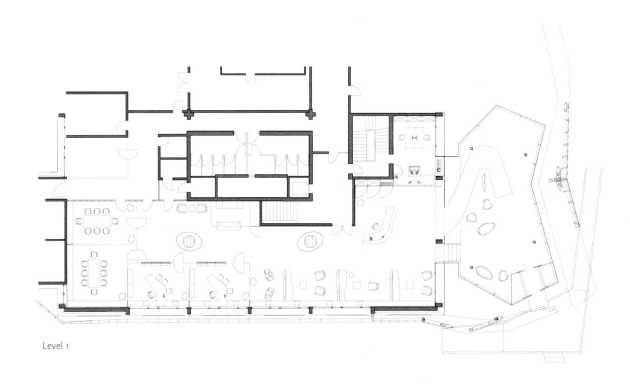

Level 1

MANITOBA HYDRO PLACE

Winnipeg, Canada   2009

This building, housing the headquarters of Manitoba Hydro, Canada's fourth-largest energy utility company, was acknowledged by the Council for Tall Buildings and Urban Habitat (CTBUH) with the award for Best Tall Building Americas.

Located in Winnipeg, one of the coldest cities in North America, the building was designed to optimize passive energy strategies and to renew 100% of the air in climate conditions where temperatures fluctuate between -23°F and 93°F, without compromising comfort for the company's close to two thousand employees.

The design, with the participation of German energy consultants Transsolar, features advanced technologies to achieve a "living building" that responds dynamically to the local climate.

The main aims of the program were: a) to create a comfortable and healthy work environment for employees; b) to obtain a 60% reduction in energy use over that of the original building; c) to revitalize the downtown area of Winnipeg, where the building is located; d) to create a 377 ft tower on the north facade to act as a solar chimney.

The final product features an exterior double facade that is biodynamic. It includes operable motorized windows programmed to open and close in response to the climate and solar glare. A new public space was also created as the result of the strategic location of the building, and designed at a 45° angle. The stairwells are finished in wood, and provide easy movement between floors, reducing elevator use.

ARCHITECT
Kuwabara Payne McKenna Blumberg Architects

CLIENT
Manitoba Hydro (Provincial Crown Corporation of Manitoba)

COLLABORATORS
Smith Carter Architects (architects of record), Transsolar (energy consultants)

TOTAL SURFACE AREA
695,000 sq ft

COST
USD 278,000,000

ENERGY CONSUMPTION
8 kWh/sq ft/year

CERTIFICATION
USGBC LEED platinum

PROGRAM
Headquarters of energy utility company

Photography © Eduard Hueber, Gerry Kopelow, Paul Hultberg

The three six-story south atria or "winter atria" serve as heat stores, in addition to being a meeting place for office workers. Waterfall features in this space humidify and dehumidify the air depending on the season.

View of the south facade

View of the north facade

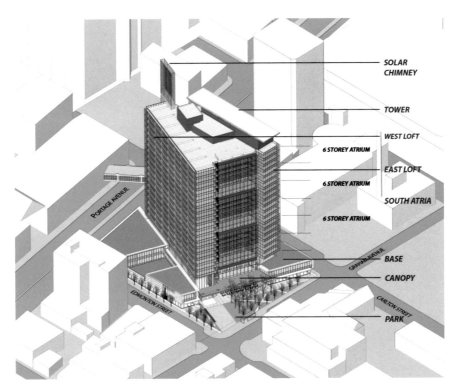

SOLAR CHIMNEY

TOWER

WEST LOFT

6 STOREY ATRIUM

EAST LOFT

6 STOREY ATRIUM

SOUTH ATRIA

6 STOREY ATRIUM

BASE

CANOPY

PARK

PORTAGE AVENUE

GRAHAM AVENUE

CARLTON STREET

EDMONTON STREET

Southwest isometric view with environmental features

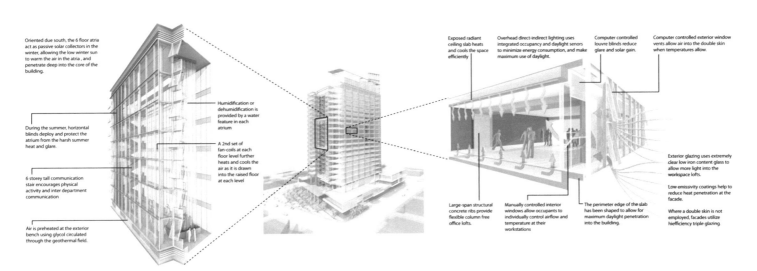

Oriented due south, the 6 floor atria act as passive solar collectors in the winter, allowing the low winter sun to warm the air in the atria , and penetrate deep into the core of the building.

During the summer, horizontal blinds deploy and protect the atrium from the harsh summer heat and glare.

6 storey tall communication stair encourages physical activity and inter department communication

Air is preheated at the exterior bench using glycol circulated through the geothermal field.

Humidification or dehumidification is provided by a water feature in each atrium

A 2nd set of fan-coils at each floor level further heats and cools the air as it is drawn into the raised floor at each level

Exposed radiant ceiling slab heats and cools the space efficiently

Overhead direct-indirect lighting uses integrated occupancy and daylight senors to minimize energy consumption, and make maximum use of daylight.

Computer controlled louvre blinds reduce glare and solar gain.

Computer controlled exterior window vents allow air into the double skin when temperatures allow.

Exterior glazing uses extremely clear low iron content glass to allow more light into the workspace lofts.

Low emissivity coatings help to reduce heat penetration at the facade.

Where a double skin is not employed, facades utilize hiefficiency triple glazing.

Large-span structural concrete ribs provide flexible column free office lofts.

Manually controlled interior windows allow occupants to individually control airflow and temperature at their workstations

The perimeter edge of the slab has been shaped to allow for maximum daylight penetration into the building.

Detailed diagram of the biodynamic facade and bioclimatic behavior of the "winter atria"

The final Comfort Tower scheme, as it was called by the architects, was meant to be a contact point or hinge for the two wings of the building on the north facade. The south facade was maintained as a solar collector and accumulator of air for cross-ventilation air-conditioning.

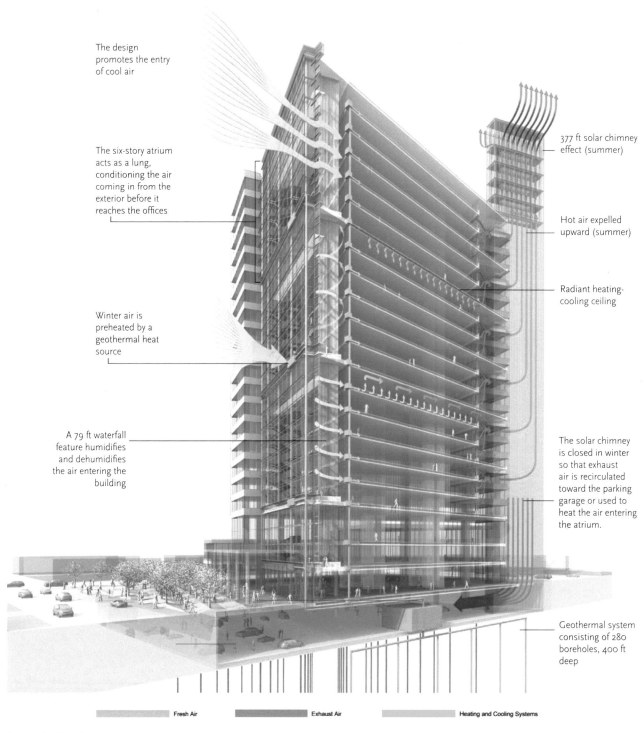

The design promotes the entry of cool air

The six-story atrium acts as a lung, conditioning the air coming in from the exterior before it reaches the offices

Winter air is preheated by a geothermal heat source

A 79 ft waterfall feature humidifies and dehumidifies the air entering the building

377 ft solar chimney effect (summer)

Hot air expelled upward (summer)

Radiant heating-cooling ceiling

The solar chimney is closed in winter so that exhaust air is recirculated toward the parking garage or used to heat the air entering the atrium.

Geothermal system consisting of 280 boreholes, 400 ft deep

Fresh Air   Exhaust Air   Heating and Cooling Systems

Seasonal airflow diagram

FREEMAN WEBB BUILDING

Nashville, TN, USA   2009

This prestigious office building was designed as part of the redevelopment project for Bedford Avenue in Green Hills, Nashville. The project was led by the Metropolitan Planning Commission and won the 2007 award by the Tennessee Chapter of the American Planning Association. This is the fourth building by the Hastings team within this development.

The building's totally rectangular volume is clad in brick with glass facades, which reduce the need for artificial lighting. It has three stories, plus a roof level and two levels of underground parking. Balcony openings feature the Energy Star–rated NanaWall retractable wall system, demonstrating that the design promotes energy savings.

The building has environmental features such as a 10,000 sq ft green roof, a high-performance operable glass skin, a high-efficiency air-conditioning and lighting system, bicycle parking spaces, and the use of recycled materials on its interior and exterior.

The quality of the building's interior is assured through the use of low-VOC paints, adhesives, and caulks. Preferred parking is for hybrid vehicles and carpoolers.

The building uses a total of 25% less energy and 30% less water than a conventional building of its type.

ARCHITECT
Hastings Architecture Associates

CLIENT
Freeman Webb Company

TOTAL SURFACE AREA
60,000 sq ft

ENERGY CONSUMPTION
1.12 kWh/sq ft/year (electricity and gas)

CERTIFICATION
USGBC LEED gold

PROGRAM
Property management headquarters

Photography © Jim Roof Creative, Inc.

The headquarters of this company, established in
1979, is the first building of its type certified LEED gold
in the state of Tennessee.

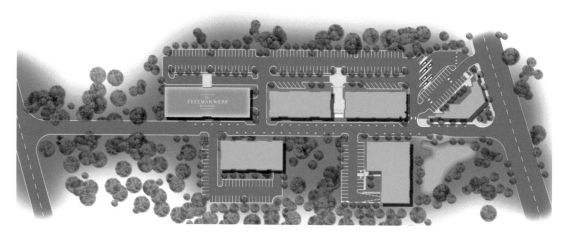

Location

West elevation

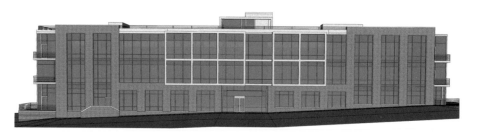

East elevation

The green roof is open to office employees and features local species of plants that require less water. The green layer retains storm water and lowers air-conditioning costs.

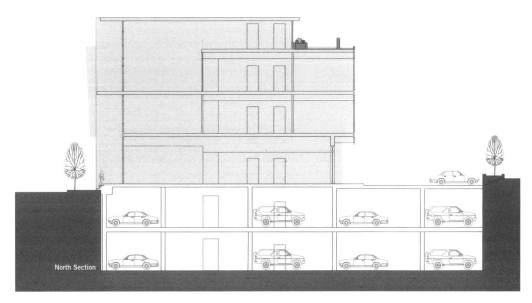

Cross-section

Color illustration of the green roof

CHILEXPRESS CORPORATE BUILDING

Santiago, Chile   2006

The new facility for this courier company consists of an office building housing the company's headquarters and an operations building with services. Both buildings are connected by means of a "meeting plaza," which is also the personnel entrance. The complex features perimeter streets and courtyards for transit and safety.

The building is a three-story horizontal volume in exposed concrete, with glass and steel curtain walls hanging away from the facades. The west facade has perforated metal panels instead of glass, which enable solar radiation to be filtered without the need for an opaque surface. The building's skin changes depending on the time of day and the viewing angle.

The combined reception and waiting area of the foyer is a double-height glazed space. Meeting and service areas are located on two sides, with the remaining space being open plan, with central transit areas and offices on the perimeter to capture natural light from the windows.

The classification and distribution center is a rectangular metal volume. It features a large open space where the automatic selection and dispatch systems are located. The building has a metal frame clad with colored vertical corrugated steel panels. The yellow serigraph windows rise the height of the building and visually resemble a barcode. They permit natural light to enter and the building's surrounding landscape to be viewed from inside.

The design of the second skins, in the form of glass curtain walls, is for technical and aesthetic effect. Being flat and at some distance from the walls of the building, they create natural vertical air circulation, which forms a thermal barrier, owing to the Venturi effect.

ARCHITECT
Guillermo Hevia/GH+A

CLIENT
Chilexpress S. A.

COLLABORATORS
Francisco Carrión G. (architect),
Marcela Suazo M. (development, CAD drawing), Alfonso Pacheco (structural calculations)

TOTAL SURFACE AREA
77,500 sq ft

COST
USD 3,805,000

ENERGY CONSUMPTION
1.6 kWh/sq ft/year (heating),
1.5 kWh/sq ft/year (cooling)

PROGRAM
Office building, operations building, and adjoining plaza

Photography © Cristián Barahona,
Guillermo Hevia

Reinforced concrete, glass, aluminum, and steel
are the principal materials in this building. The roof
and cladding consist of prefabricated metal sheets
that were prepainted the color of stainless steel and
insulated on the underside with polyurethane.

Elevations

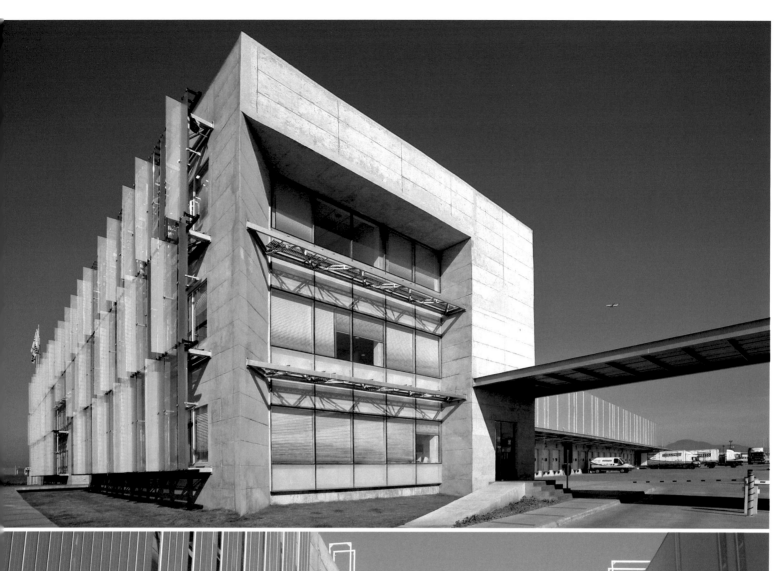

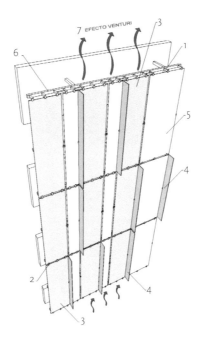

1. 2x2 in galvanized metal frame members
2. Metal support
3. Satin tempered glass
4. Tempered glass serigraphed yellow
5. Clear tempered glass
6. 3.15x3.15 in galvanized metal frame members
7. Venturi effect

Detail of the east facade with Venturi effect

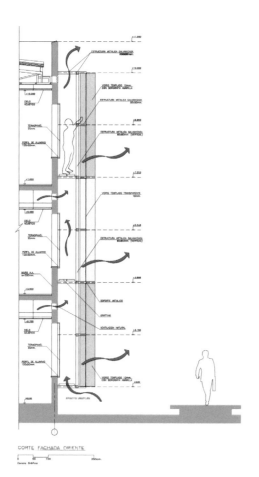

Section east facade (glass)

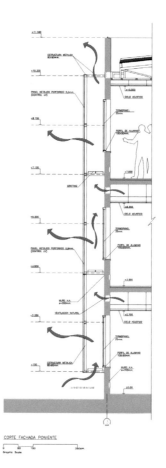

Section west facade (perforated metal)

This new international courier company has
34,500 sq ft dedicated to administration and services
and 43,000 sq ft to dispatch operations.

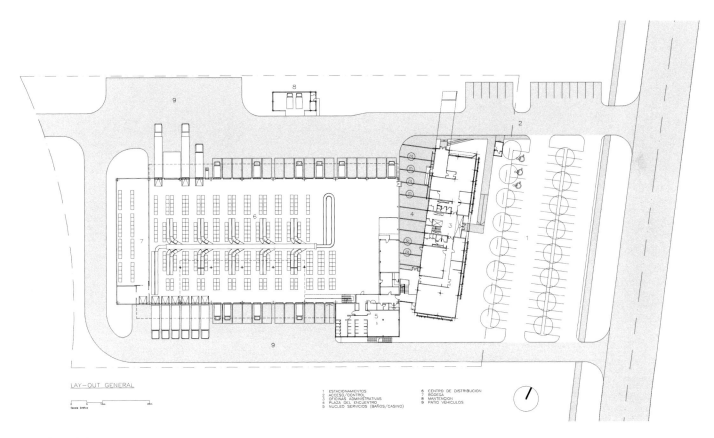

LAY-OUT GENERAL

1 ESTACIONAMIENTOS
2 ACCESO/CONTROL
3 OFICINAS ADMINISTRATIVAS
4 PLAZA DEL ENCUENTRO
5 NUCLEO SERVICIOS (BAÑOS/CASINO)

6 CENTRO DE DISTRIBUCION
7 BODEGA
8 MANTENCION
9 PATIO VEHICULOS

Ground plan

GAES HEADQUARTERS

Barcelona, Spain   2009

GAES is an example of a high-technology industry perfectly integrated with a city. Its production process calls for lab coats and microscopes. There is no waste or noise, and no heavy machinery is required. Product manufacturing coexists in the same building as the sales department, administration, R&D, marketing, and management, to allow for a hybrid center of knowledge, production, and sales.

The facade is a living facade and features a double skin, with moving louvers changing position depending on the location of the sun and weather conditions. A system of automated funnels connected to a weather station and a hidden system of motors keeps the facade in movement.

This skin, which is ventilated and flexible, is colored in different shades of green, and provides a softened but full view of the local landscape from the inside. It also filters 30% of solar radiation.

The building participates in citywide environmental strategies in the context of its location in the 22@ district. Integral waste management is carried out by means of a network of pneumatic tubes connecting each building with a central recycling and waste management plant. Similarly, the cooling and hot water systems are integrated with a district cooling and heating distribution network. This network is mainly powered by residual steam from a waste incineration plant.

ARCHITECT
Mizien Arquitectura, G56

CLIENT
GAES

COLLABORATORS
BOMA (structural consultant), G56 Ingeniería (services consultant), Biosca & Botey, COLT (facade consultant)

TOTAL SURFACE AREA
63,500 sq ft

COST
USD 10,850,000

ENERGY CONSUMPTION
9 kWh/sq ft/year

PROGRAM
Offices, laboratories, and R&D facilities for the manufacturing of hearing aids

Photography © Eugeni Pons

The glass louvers move between two extreme
positions: fully closed, appearing as a continuous
glass expanse, and fully open. The almost-closed
position protects against the summer sun.

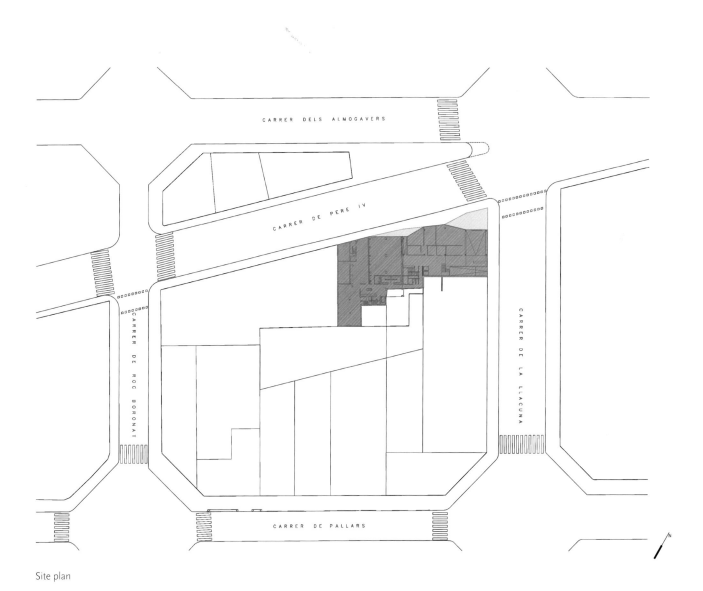

Site plan

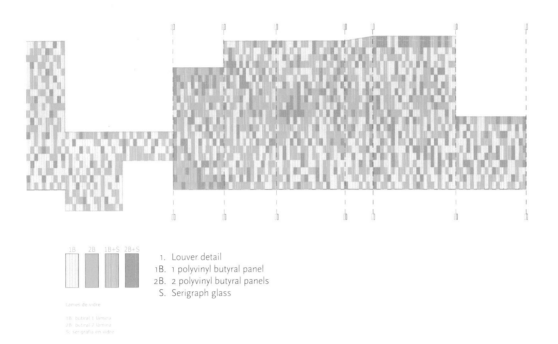

1B 2B 1B+S 2B+S

1. Louver detail
1B. 1 polyvinyl butyral panel
2B. 2 polyvinyl butyral panels
S. Serigraph glass

Lames de vidre

1B. butiral 1 làmina
2B. butiral 2 làmina
S. serigrafia en vidre

Facade detail and glass louver positioning diagram

There is a 28 in separation between the inner skin and the primary skin, creating a chamber that can be accessed by maintenance and cleaning personnel. The glass has insulating properties and low emissivity. The facade combines the automated louver control with a manual control.

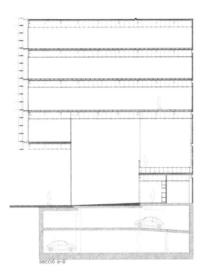

A-A cross section

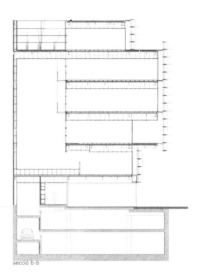

B-B cross section

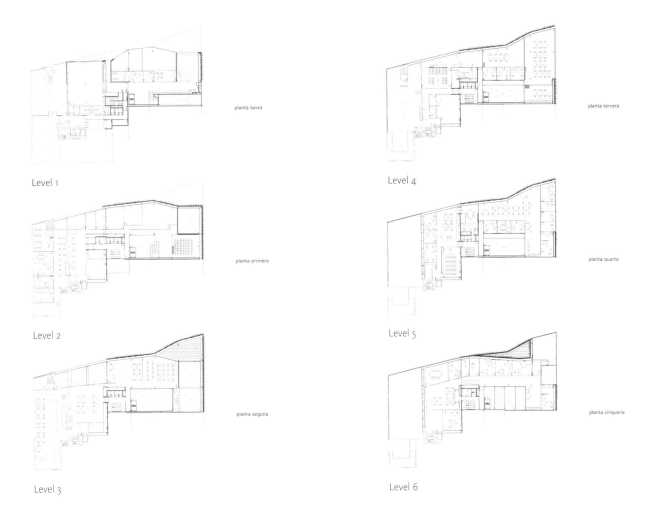

Level 1 — planta baixa

Level 2 — planta primera

Level 3 — planta segona

Level 4 — planta tercera

Level 5 — planta quarta

Level 6 — planta cinquena

THE NEW YORK TIMES BUILDING

New York, NY, USA   2007

This fifty-two story building is shared by Forest City Ratner Companies (FCRC), with twenty-nine floors plus retail space, and the New York Times Company, with twenty-seven floors.

Renzo Piano designed an innovative double skin for the building, which features ceramic rods on the exterior of a glass curtain wall that acts as a screen to lessen the effects of solar gain on the building. The curtain wall, which deflects the heat it receives, allows a view of the building's surroundings to be enjoyed from inside, without it being totally opaque from the street. The use of ceramic rods creates effects with the changing light during the day.

The Lawrence Berkeley National Laboratory helped design a regulable lighting system, in addition to a selective dynamic shade that produces energy savings of 30%. The systems of lighting controls can be controlled individually in each space. A cogeneration plant produces energy on-site and supplies 40% of the building's energy needs.

A versatile heating system provides underfloor air distribution, which also creates cool air 18 degrees lower than conventional systems at 68°F. Hot air is extracted through vents in the ceiling. This system also takes advantage of cold morning air on the exterior to generate cool air, and also uses the residual heat from the cogeneration plant.

The eighteen thousand lighting points in the building can be programmed individually to meet the needs of each department. More than 95% of the structural steel has a recycled component.

ARCHITECT
Renzo Piano Building Workshop, FXFOWLE Architects

CLIENT
The New York Times Company (TNYTC) and Forest City Ratner Companies (FCRC)

COLLABORATORS
Gensler (interior design), Thornton Tomasetti (structural engineering), Flack + Kurtz (mechanical, electrical, and fluid engineering), AMEC Construction Management, Inc. (construction), Turner Construction (interior design)

TOTAL SURFACE AREA
800,000 sq ft (TNYTC), 700,000 sq ft (FCRC), 21,000 sq ft (retail space)

COST
USD 640,000,000

PROGRAM
TNYTC and FCRC headquarters

Photography © David Sundberg/ESTO, Nic Lehoux

This building incorporates many of the defining features in Renzo Piano's architecture: volume, views, transparency, respect for setting, and permeability.

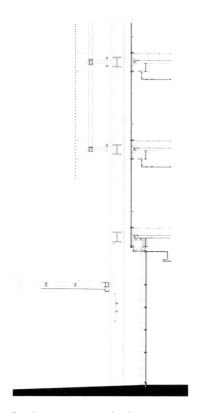

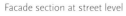

Facade section at street level

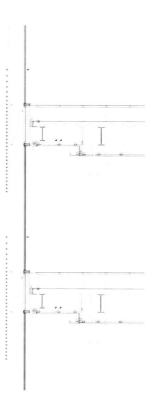

Typical facade section on higher floors

The New York Times offices are designed to be flexible
and changeable spaces. For this purpose, they have an
open-plan layout, with plenty of space for meetings and
interdepartmental collaborations.

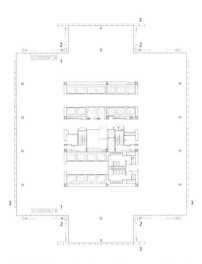

Typical floor plan (from 18th to 22nd floors)

41ST STREET

8TH AVENUE

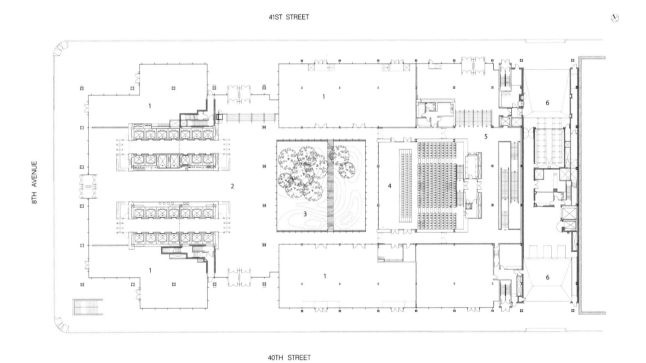

40TH STREET

First floor

BENDIGO BANK HEADQUARTERS

Bendigo, Victoria, Australia
2007 (stages I and II) – 2008 (stage III)

With a workforce of nine hundred people in Bendigo and the surrounding area, Bendigo and Adelaide Bank's management decided to combine the offices and personnel of the five different locations it ran its operations from.

More than being a corporate symbol, the design of the new office was meant to serve the community. The architectural brief included abundant natural light, integration of the project into the urban fabric of the heritage precinct of the Bendigo business district, encouragement of informal interaction between employees, and a building with a small carbon footprint.

A sense of community is achieved with retail areas on the first floor and extensive public spaces, including a new public square. In order to blend with the urban landscape, the building does not dominate the Bendigo skyline. For this reason, it only has four levels of office space and a fifth level for housing plant and service installations, all of which are located above the retail floor (first level) and the parking area (mezzanine).

The facades were designed to respond to the orientation of each frontage. The west frontage is adorned with colored perforated aluminum sunshades. The sunshades reduce the harsh western sun while the facade serves as thermal mass.

The atriums, corridors, and internal walkways were designed to reinforce an individual and departmental sense of identity despite the building's dimensions. Environmental features include atriums for natural light, insulated glazing, external sunshade, insulation that increases thermal mass, solar thermal panels, and tools for rainwater collection, wastewater recycling, interior air renewal, and CO_2 level control.

ARCHITECT
Gray Puksand + BVN Architecture

CLIENT
Bendigo Bank, Fountain Plaza Landlord Pty Ltd

TOTAL SURFACE AREA
150,700 sq ft of offices, 21,530 sq ft of retail space

COST
USD 71,000,000

ENERGY CONSUMPTION
7.5 kWh/sq ft/year

CERTIFICATION
5 Star Green Star – Office Design v1

PROGRAM
Bank head office

Photography © John Gollings, Dianna Snape

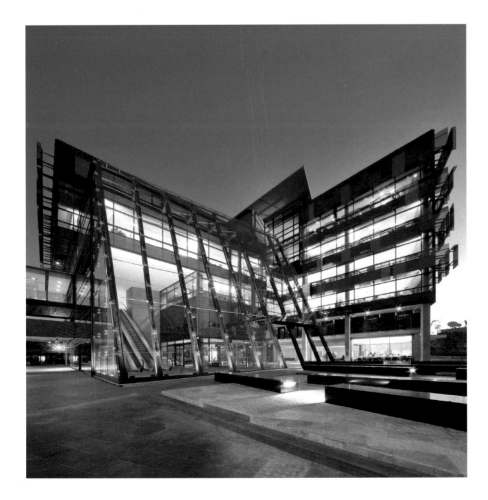

Protection from the sun, especially on the west facade, consists of perforated sunshades positioned 6 ft away from the wall. The perforations and positioning of these screens were designed to reduce solar gain and glare while maximizing views.

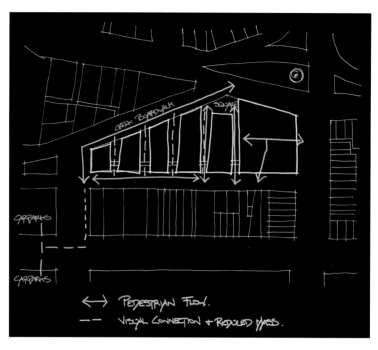

Plan of transit areas and potential visibility

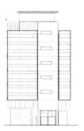

South elevation

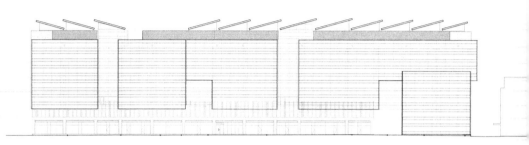

East elevation

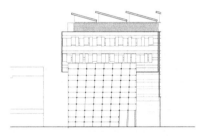

West elevation (building 5)

West elevation

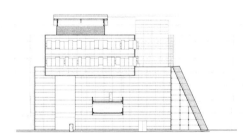

North elevation (building 5)

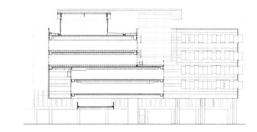

North elevation (building 4)

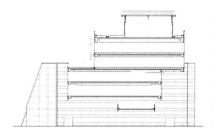

South elevation (building 5)

The design plan made sure every workstation is no
farther than 26 ft away from natural light. The intensity
of light in communal areas is 150 lux; the offices
typically have 320 lux.

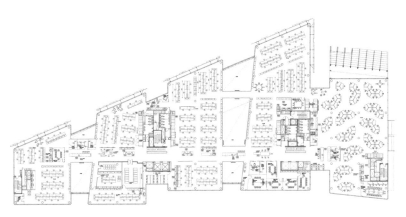

Third level

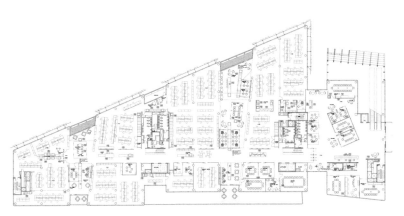

Second level

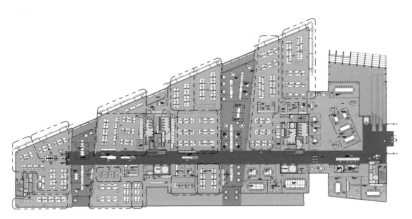

First level

Fifth level

Fourth level

WWF NETHERLANDS HEAD OFFICE

Zeist, Netherlands   2006

RAU turned this former agricultural laboratory into a carbon-neutral building, with close to zero CO_2 emissions. The new design breaks with the rigidity of the original building, adds an amorphous space at the center of the building, and gives it new life.

Some parts of the old laboratory were demolished, returning the previously occupied spaces to a natural state. The land surrounding the new building was turned into a biotope, providing birds and bats with nesting places.

The renovation replaced much of the concrete, predominant in the original building, with natural materials. A large degree of the building's facades are glassed in order to enable natural light to enter. The walls and roof of the building are lined with mud, which, besides absorbing humidity, is good thermal insulation. Floor coverings are made from recycled tire inner tubes.

One of the most outstanding features of this project is the building's energy efficiency, based on triple-pane insulated glazing and wood louvers to protect from harmful radiation. There are also photovoltaic panels and solar thermal panels to heat water. Heaters and air-conditioning are not necessary in this building. The heat generated inside the building is captured and reused. Excess summer heat is stored in an underground water reservoir and used to heat the building in winter. Cold energy is stored underground in winter and used to cool the building in summer.

ARCHITECT
RAU

CLIENT
WWF Netherlands

TOTAL SURFACE AREA
40,900 sq ft

COST
USD 5,400,000

CERTIFICATION
EPBD A++ European Union,
GreenCalc 269

PROGRAM
Head office for WWF Netherlands

Photography © Kusters Fotografie,
Hans Lebbe, RAU

All timber used on facades and interior finishes and furnishings is FSC-certified. Interior air quality, with a low level of allergens and suspended particles, is assured through the use of natural materials and cross-ventilation.

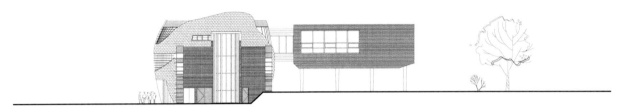

Side elevation

Longitudinal elevation

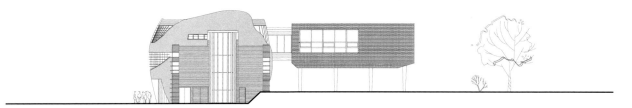

Cross-section (central core)

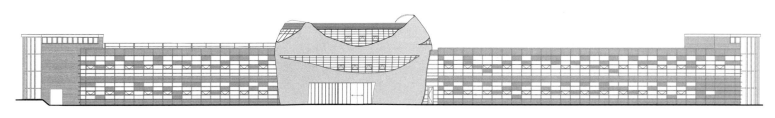

Longitudinal section (central core)

There is a flexible floor plan, and all public areas, such as the reception area, the call center, the store, and meeting rooms, are laid out around the stairwell. Light entering through the glazed facades enhances the open feel of the spaces.

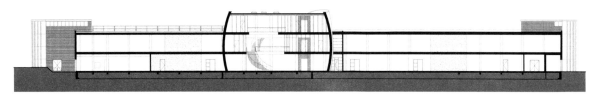

A-A section

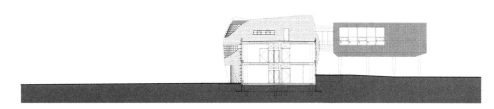

B-B section

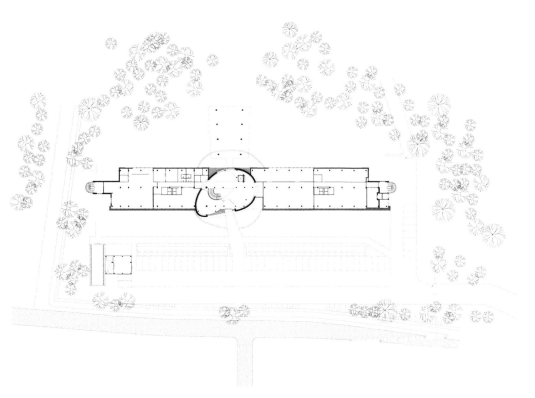

Ground plan

UNILEVER HEADQUARTERS FOR GERMANY, AUSTRIA, AND SWITZERLAND

Hamburg, Germany 2009

This building was designed to house the twelve hundred employees of Unilever, a company operating in the agrifood and personal hygiene sectors. It is located on the banks of the Elbe River in Hamburg, and is the new headquarters of Unilever for Germany, Austria, and Switzerland.

The building is part of the redeveloped HafenCity area, a redevelopment of the old industrial port area of Hamburg, and it is close to the cruise ship terminal and the Strandkai pedestrian promenade. It is laid out over nine levels, two of them underground, and has four hundred parking spaces.

The key aspect of the design is the central atrium, which gets flooded with natural daylight. It is open to passersby, who can shop at the Unilever store on the first floor, sit in a coffee shop, or relax at the spa. For those working in the build-ing, the atrium is also a place to meet and communicate. Like an inner city, a series of bridges, ramps, and stairs connect this central area with other areas and levels.

The building's bioclimatic design re-jects the use of technical solutions wher-ever possible. The offices are cooled by means of thermally activated reinforced concrete ceilings. A second skin placed in front of the glass facade protects the interior from inclement weather events like wind and rain. The building features an innovative SMD-LED lighting system, 70% more efficient than halogen or metal halide lighting, and allows natural lighting to be enhanced in all areas,

Mechanical ventilation systems func-tions by compressing filtered air through the floors. The atrium has a heat exchang-er at its highest point to recover heat from the used air before extracting it.

ARCHITECT
Behnisch Architekten

CLIENT
Strandkai 1 Projekt GmbH

COLLABORATORS
360grad+ (supervision), Weber Poll (structural engineering), HKP Ingenieure GmbH (mechanical and electrical engineering), Transsolar (energy consultant), ITA Weimar (insulation and acoustics), Horstmann + Berger (building physics consultant), EMBT Enric Miralles – Benedetta Tagliabue (landscaping)

TOTAL SURFACE AREA
410,000 sq ft

CERTIFICATION
Gold HafenCity Ecolabel

PROGRAM
Mixed-use corporate building (offices, conference centers, coffee shops, restaurants, and retail space)

Photography © Adam Mørk

Every workstation has operable windows that can be controlled individually. A double-facade system, comprising a glass skin and an EFTE one, provides ventilation to spaces by means of the circulation of air between the two.

Rendering

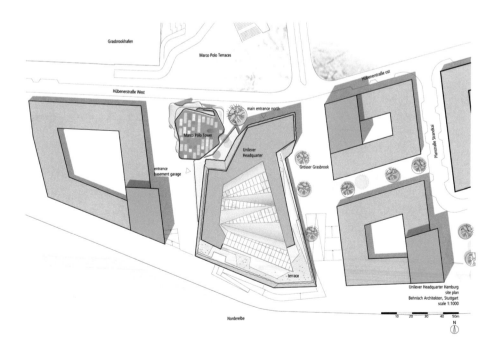

Site plan

In the interior, use has been made of materials free
from halogens, volatile compounds, and biocides.
The solid timber used has been certified by competent
authorities.

1. Terrace
2. Meeting point
3. Parking
4. LED luminaries
5. Reception
6. Offices
7. North entrance

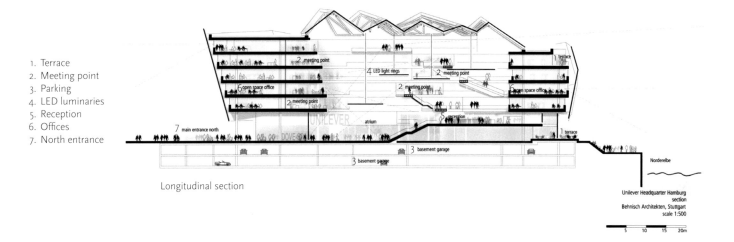

Longitudinal section

Unilever Headquarter Hamburg
section
Behnisch Architekten, Stuttgart
scale 1:500

1. Filter
2. Hot air extraction

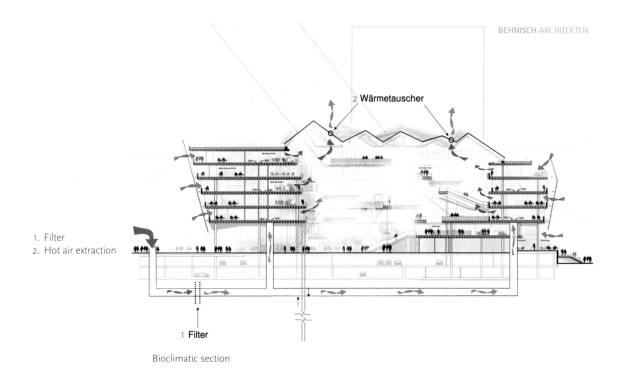

Bioclimatic section

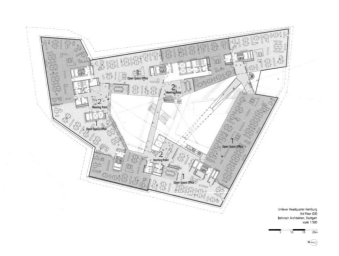

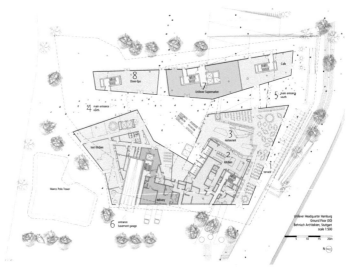

Level 4   1. Offices
                 2. Meeting point

First floor   1. Terrace   5. South entrance
                  2. Kitchen   6. Parking entrance
                  3. Restaurant   7. Store
                  4. North entrance   8. Spa

RESIDENTIAL COMPLEX

SCHLIERBERG RESIDENTIAL COMPLEX

Freiburg, Germany   2006

This residential complex was built in the early years of this century and is a helpful starting point for tracing the current popularity of eco districts and green urban planning. Awarded with the first prize in the Öko 2000 competition by the German Ministry for the Environment, Nature Conservation, and Nuclear Safety, this project was a key solar energy initiative featured at EXPO 2000 in Hannover. The program consists of fifty-nine housing units, including nine penthouses over a building with retail and office uses, that Rolf Disch considers to fulfill *Plusenergiehaus* plus-energy-house) requirements—this term showing that they generate more energy than they need. All of the buildings face south, and the distance between the rows of townhouses was calculated to make the most of the winter sun, which is much lower on the horizon than the summer sun.

Most of the homes have two or three stories, and there are communal facilities. The complex is well served by the local public transport network, and there is a good system of pedestrian walkways and bike paths.

The aim of this pioneering complex was to generate enough solar energy for communal use by the residents. Heating and hot water are provided by hot water tanks warmed with solar energy, and also with power from a woodchip-fueled biomass plant. Surplus energy can be sold to the national grid. It is estimated that at least 65 cents/kWh will be made from sold electricity during the twenty useful years of the system.

ARCHITECT
Rolf Disch Solar Architecture

CLIENT
Solarsiedlung GmbH

GROSS FLOOR AREA
72,600 sq ft of townhouses, 12,500 sq ft of penthouses atop an adjacent building

ENERGY CONSUMPTION
Surplus of 3.3 kWh/sq ft/year (generates more energy than needed)

PROGRAM
Residential complex with renewable energy systems

Photography © Ramesh Amruth, Georg Nemec

The wall coverings and the barely treated light metal frames reflect the goals of model experimental urban design prototypes: to use research to create new ways of living that have lower carbon footprints than conventional ways of living.

The predominant use of metal on exteriors contrasts
with the interiors, which have light-colored wood on
walls and surfaces. The flooring is made of natural
materials, and much of it is made from varnished cork.

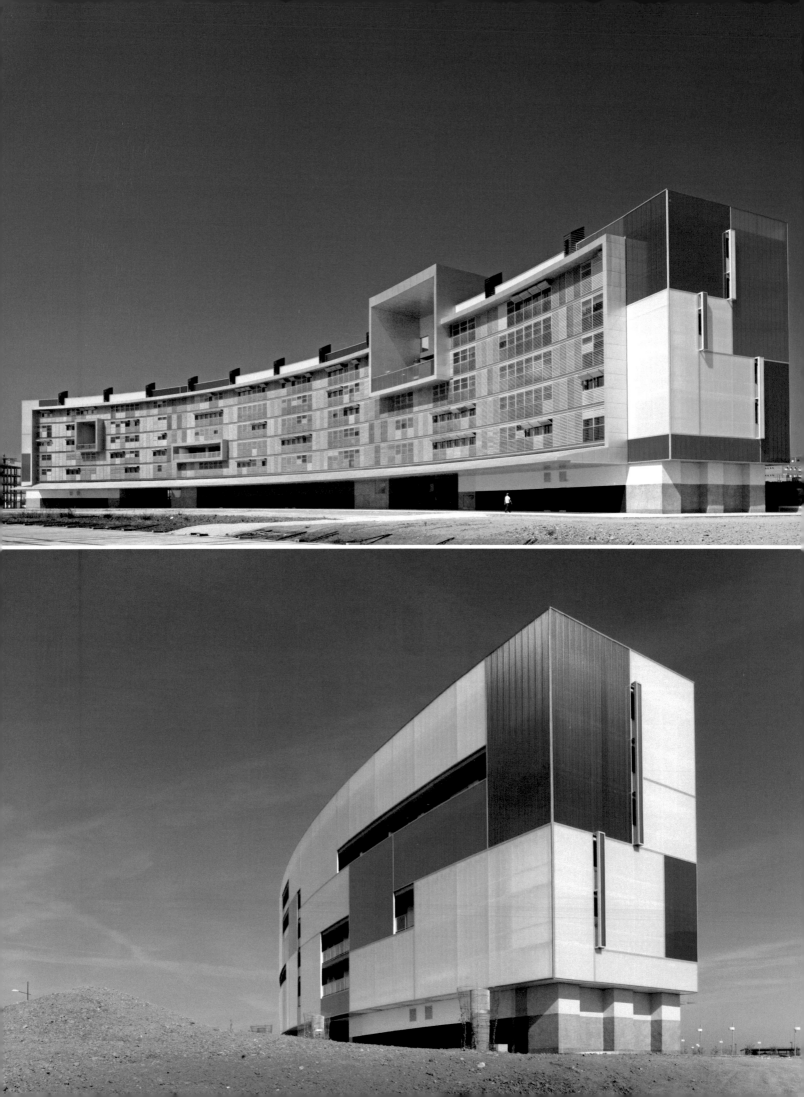

HEMICICLO SOLAR

Móstoles, Spain   2009

This building contains ninety-two subsidized rental apartments for young people, with 10,800 sq ft of retail space and basement parking. The design sought to follow high-energy-efficiency criteria while providing spaces to integrate groups of different cultural, social, and ethnic backgrounds.

The podium separates public uses from private, enabling the first level to act like a filter between the plaza and the north-facing green spaces.

The skin is an essential feature. On the south side, it enables the building to make use of solar radiation as energy by means of a series of glassed balcony spaces that use the greenhouse effect to accumulate heat like actual solar heaters during winter. This system is a complement to the wall radiators, which are fed from a low-energy central boiler.

The building's glass spaces are protected from the summer sun by regulable louvers. A system of buried conduits was designed to provide the building with renewed air throughout the year, and this functions as a passive cooling system in summer, an alternative to mechanical air-conditioning.

In compliance with the Spanish building code for domestic hot water, an array of fifty-five solar thermal panels was designed for the south-facing porch on the first floor. Over an average building of similar size and layout, the energy balance shows a 49% saving in energy consumption, 75% saving in greenhouse gas emissions, and 46% environmental comfort level.

ARCHITECT
Ruiz-Larrea & Asociados

CLIENT
Instituto Municipal del Suelo de Móstoles

COLLABORATORS
IMSM (quantity surveyor), FATECSA (construction), NB35 (structure), ELIA Solar (bioclimatic consultant), Javier Neila (bioclimatic architect, Polytechnic University of Madrid)

HABITABLE SURFACE AREA
68,000 sq ft

COST
USD 15,900,000

CERTIFICATION
B+ (EU building energy performance certification)

PROGRAM
Bioclimatic building containing 92 public housing units, retail space, and parking

Photography © Angel Baltanás

This block is south facing and lightly curved to
enhance solar energy capture, like a parabolic reflector,
from which it takes its name.

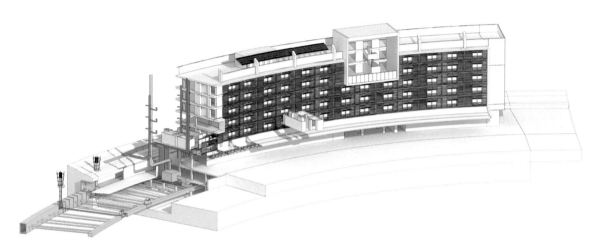

Diagram

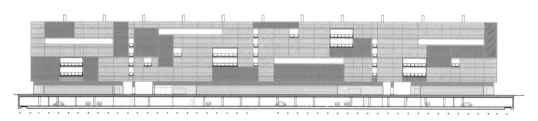

North elevation

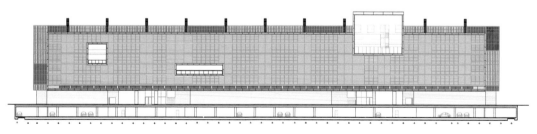

South elevation

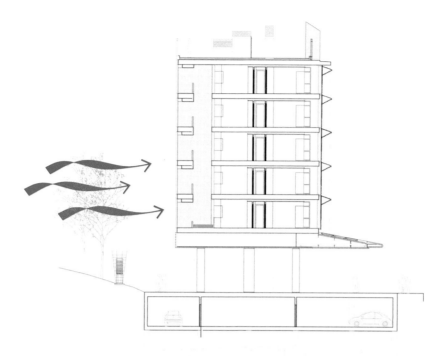

Cool breeze capture through the north facade (summer)

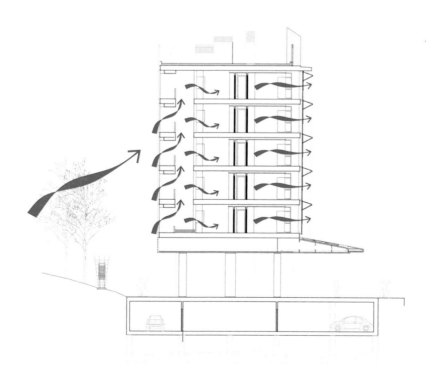

Night ventilation (dual-aspect units) in summer

Passive energy-saving systems provide cross-ventilation for apartments in summer through openings on both sides.

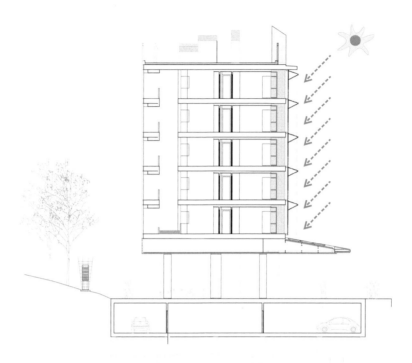

Solar radiation capture through glazed balcony (winter)

Summer-winter energy polarity

Level 6

Level 4

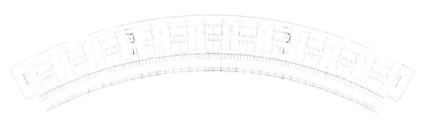

Level 2

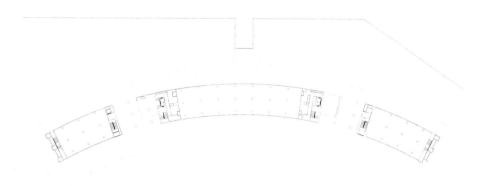

Level 1

LUCIEN ROSE COMPLEX

Rennes, France   2004

Atelier du Pont, member of the PLAN01 collective, was commissioned to develop this program consisting of eighty-one public housing units (70,000 sq ft in total) and an 8,580 sq ft public library.

Located in the Thabor Botanical Gardens district, an upper-middle-class area in Rennes, the plan included the construction of a new public library and new entrances to Thabor Park, in addition to the public housing project and parking. As the project involved public housing, the developers did have concerns that it would become a ghetto of working class residents in the midst of a wealthier community.

The residential complex comprises six buildings combining townhouses and apartment blocks. The geometry and color scheme of the complex blends seamlessly with the existing park.

The apartments are organized into six separate areas. Three blocks border the northern limit, adjoining the park. They are visually integrated because of their second skin, made of vertical timber slats. Their shaded balconies face south and offer views of the city of Rennes.

The library is separated from the residential buildings, but it has a contemporary feel, made using simple and elegant-looking materials. Outside the library, one can enter Thabor Park through nineteenth-century wrought iron gates. Inside, the gray floors and interior walls contrast with bright red bands and the clean lines of furnishings. The suspended ceiling of perforated steel permits the entry of warm light through three skylights. The library foyer is often used as an exhibition space. The reading room is on the second level and offices are on the third.

ARCHITECT
Atelier du Pont

CLIENT
City of Rennes (library) and Archipel Habitat (public housing)

COLLABORATORS
EVP (structural engineering), OFI (fluid engineering), and Ronand Desorneaux (landscaping)

TOTAL SURFACE AREA
78,580 sq ft

COST
USD 12,300,000

ENERGY CONSUMPTION
6.4 kWh/sq ft/year

PROGRAM
81-unit public housing development and public library

Photography © Luc Boegly

The new housing development is located on one side of Thabor Park, a green space in a residential neighborhood of downtown Rennes. The double wood facade on the north side of the apartment blocks allows them to visually merge with the park.

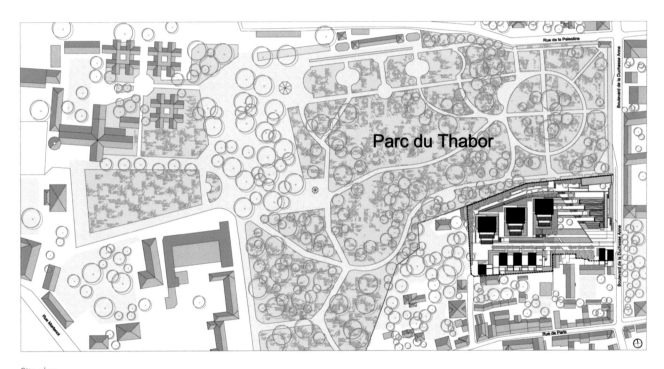

Site plan

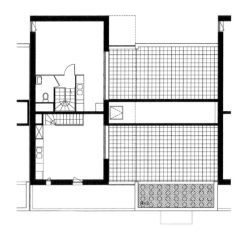 

Type B building floor plan

The complex combines townhouses with multiple-
residence buildings in keeping with low-density
principles so that the internal transit areas are not
overcrowded.

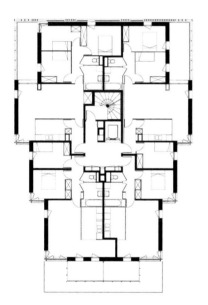

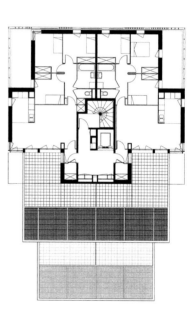

Type C building floor plan

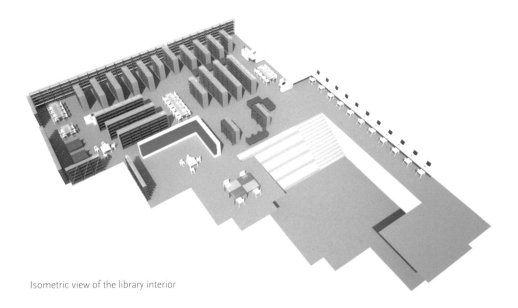

Isometric view of the library interior

WAKERING ROAD FOYER

London, United Kingdom   2009

This residence is built on 18,000 sq ft of land formerly occupied by a parking lot in the district of Barking. It is located near a busy road and rail transport. With 116 beds, it houses disadvantaged young people between the ages of sixteen and twenty-five—young parents, rehabilitated drug addicts, and those with physical and mental disabilities. They spend a maximum of two years here before returning to their homes.

An L-shaped complex, Wakering Road Foyer is made up of one two-story block and another nine-story building, which has a covered outdoor space on the first level and a roof terrace above. The nine-story tower's first and second levels contain administration offices. It is bisected by a glazed circulation "spine." This wing contains training rooms and communal spaces such as the laundry and a day care center, in addition to apartments.

The taller block is clad in precast glass-fiber reinforced concrete (GFRC) panels. The lower wing features a curtain wall in clear, translucent, and opaque glass. The tower cladding is an abstract composition of vertical panels that hide the dull and repetitive nature of the apartments. Colored glass fins cast colored shadows across the facades.

The complex is heated and cooled by means of a geothermal pump, to which a heat-recovery ventilation system has been added. Gray water from apartment showers is recycled for use in toilets. Parts of the building, such as the toilet modules, are prefabricated.

The complex is certified by EcoHomes, which is a version of the BREEAM (BRE Environmental Assessment Method) for new or remodeled homes, individual homes, or residential developments.

ARCHITECT
Jestico + Whiles

CLIENT
East Thames Group

COLLABORATORS
Conisbee (structural engineering), Atelier Ten, Waterstone Design, (building services engineering), Robert Lombardelli Partnership (project manager), Galliford Try (contractor)

TOTAL SURFACE AREA
69,000 sq ft

COST
USD 26,570,000

ENERGY CONSUMPTION
5.5 kWh/sq ft/year (offices only)

CERTIFICATION
EcoHomes—BREEAM Very Good

PROGRAM
Residence for disadvantaged young people

Photography © Nikhilesh Haval

The roof garden atop the lower wing is for the use of
residents and employees, with an area reserved for the
adjoining day care center. This space is considered a
rest area and an oasis in the midst of a busy district.

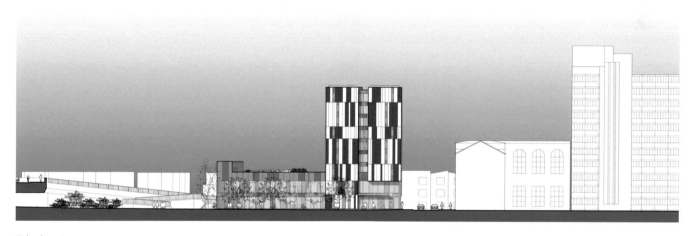

Side elevation

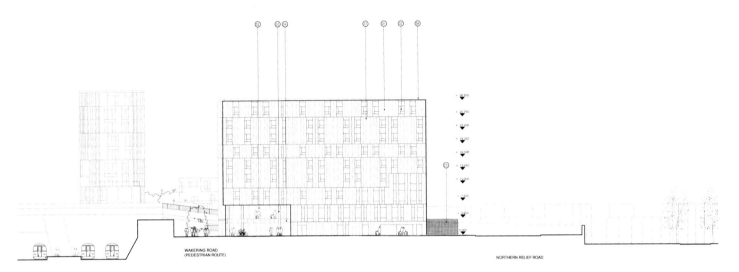

Southeast elevation

WAKERING ROAD
(PEDESTRIAN ROUTE)

NORTHERN RELIEF ROAD

The entrance is through a double-height glass reception area at the junction of the two different walkways running through the interior. There is no on-site parking for cars except for two disabled spaces, although space is provided for bicycles.

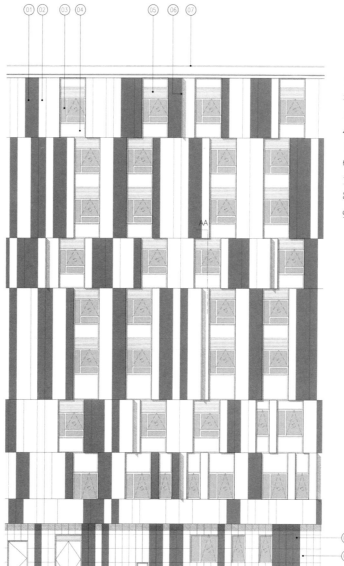

1. Anthracite GFRC panel
2. Ivory GFRC panel
3. Double-glazed aluminum joinery
4. Insulated opaque panel
5. Aluminum sun shade
6. Colored glass fins
7. Metal profile
8. Gray recycled ceramic wall covering
9. Ivory recycled ceramic wall covering

Wakering Road Frontage

IRONHORSE

Oakland, CA, USA 2010

This complex is located at the heart of an urban development plan covering twenty-nine acres of former industrial land. It is part of the Central Station master plan that envisages the construction of twelve hundred homes, with participation from different developers, together with a retail district and the restoration of Oakland's historic Sixteenth Street Station.

This specific development comprises ninety-nine apartments in a series of four-story buildings laid out around a main courtyard, as well as a freestanding community pavilion. Residents enter the complex through an open-air lobby, and units overlook the landscaped courtyard.

The east and west frontages of the complex are designed differently to respond to the spatial limitations of the complex, the existence of townhouses on one of its sides and a highway on its other.

The project has been awarded a Green Point Rating certification by the Build It Green organization, having twice the number of requisites needed. Among the environmental features that allowed it this rating are:
- Green roofs acting as thermal and acoustic insulation
- Thermal solar panels
- Photovoltaic panels (130 kW) supplying energy to communal areas
- CRI Green Label Plus certified carpets
- Outdoor furnishings made from reused wood
- Remote control watering, the use of which is dependent on information provided by a meteorological satellite
- High-efficiency drip irrigation system
- Two landscaped drainage systems that naturally filter rainwater captured on the roof to the water table.

ARCHITECT
David Baker + Partners

CLIENT
Bridge Housing

COLLABORATORS
PGA Design (landscaping), Horton Lees Brogden (lighting), Murphy Burr Curry (structural engineering), FW Associates (electrical engineering), SJ Engineers (mechanical and plumbing engineering), Sun Light & Power (solar contractor), J. H. Fitzmaurice, Inc. (contractor), Sandis (civil engineering)

TOTAL SURFACE AREA
153,395 sq ft

COST
USD 41,400,000

ENERGY CONSUMPTION
6 kWh/sq ft/year

CERTIFICATION
Build It Green GreenPoint certification

PROGRAM
Public housing development with 99 apartments

Photography © David Baker + Partners

The project features a functional design and different color schemes depending on the type of housing block and on the location of units on the interior or exterior of the complex.

Rendering

The main courtyard and freshly planted green roof on
the community pavilion.

Above: the entrance to the complex from the
Fourteenth Street lobby. Below: the pedestrian mews
separating the Ironhorse complex from the Pacific
Cannery Lofts. The metal planter boxes are offered to
residents for use as personal vegetable gardens.

280

Basement level

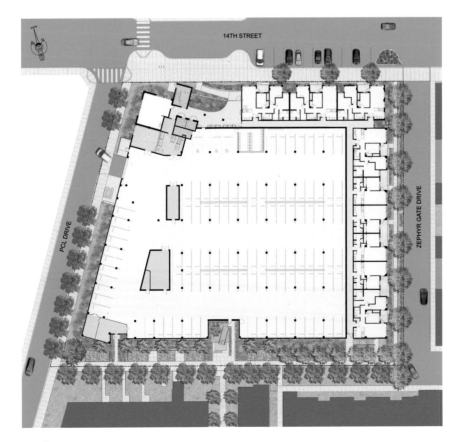

First floor

LOLOMAS

Clovis, NM, USA   2009

This program planned a residential development containing fifty-five townhouses for families and individuals, with a bioclimatic design that would minimize energy needs and maintenance requirements. The complex consists of thirty-six two-bedroom housing units (860 sq ft each), nineteen one-bedroom units, and a communal space for residents. Townhouses are grouped together in three-house modules, consisting of two family units and one one-bedroom unit.

The energy system is defined by two basic elements: south-facing glass facades that act as solar collectors, and interior thermal mass, (concrete floor slabs) that store heat during the day then release it for overnight warming.

The buildings are south facing. The windows are fitted with interior levered sunshades to prevent overheating in summer. The design encourages cross-ventilation throughout each unit by its arrangement of regulable skylights and windows. The complex also makes use of active strategies such as wind turbines and battery-powered support systems.

All of the homes are brick, with perforated facades. The complex is laid out as a series of ribs bordered by brick walls emerging from a central transit area. The complex is designed with pedestrian needs in mind, and is in walking distance of areas with grocery stores, restaurants, and churches.

ARCHITECT
Rockhill and Associates

CLIENT
Tierra Realty Trust

COLLABORATORS
Van Amburgh and Pares

HABITABLE SURFACE AREA
214,000 sq ft

COST
USD 7,628,000

ENERGY CONSUMPTION
9.3 kWh/sq ft/year

CERTIFICATION
Green Communities Criteria

PROGRAM
55-unit residential development

Photography © Patrick Coulie Photography

The uniformity of the complex is accentuated by two repeating elements—the brick dividing walls and the mesh fences. There are also concrete walkways between each three-unit module, which run perpendicular to the central walkway and divide the complex down the middle.

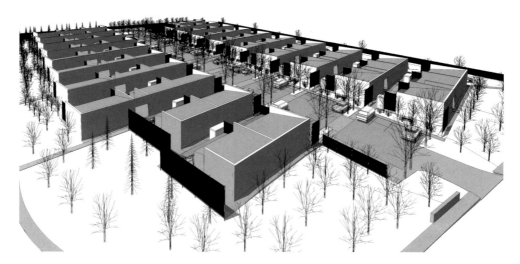

3-D view

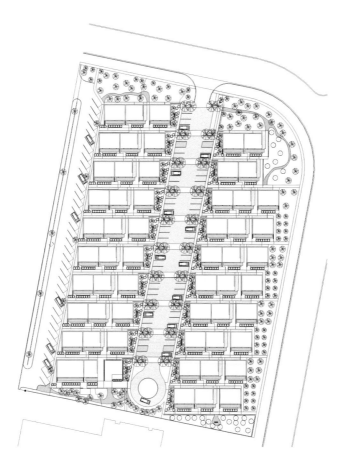

Ground plan

The layout of the complex is based on the sun being the source of energy and aims to reduce the use of fossil fuels.

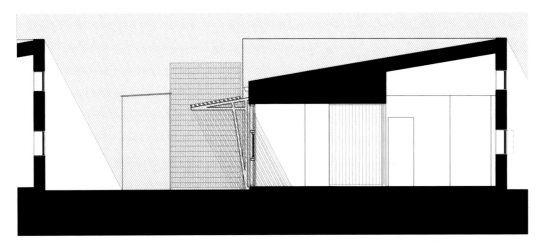

Bioclimatic diagram (summer)

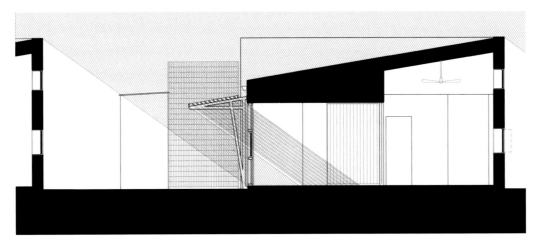

Bioclimatic diagram (winter)

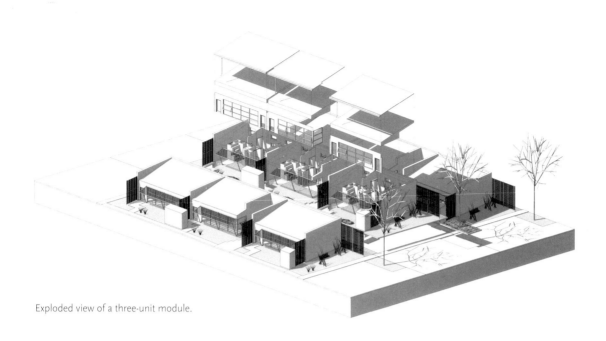

Exploded view of a three-unit module.

Detailed ground plan

EDEN BIO

Paris, France   2008

The program consists of ninety-eight public housing units with fifty-two parking spaces and eleven spaces for use as communal spaces or artists' studios. According to the architect, this project is a radical contemporary response to what he considers to be an outdated urban fabric—the picturesque working-class district of Vignoles consists of a series of narrow lanes about two yards across.

Edouard François shows a preference for buildings of differing heights and voids rather than traditional two-story buildings. The complex is a contextual patchwork of red shingles, timber pillars, zinc, flowerpots, copper, whitewashed plaster, and coarse-textured concrete. The development is laid out as a rectangle and will be overgrown with different plant and vine species in a space of five years. These have already become entwined around the stairways.

François specializes in plant wall systems (green facades and "living" walls), which he creates by means of a latticed scaffold or trellis that rises from the ground and around which vines can entwine as they grow upward. The time required for completion of a wall depends on the plants reaching the top to create a full green filter.

The architect made use of the organic soil substrate used in ecological farming, and the plants came from certified nurseries. Plant species were chosen for their ability to thrive without fertilizers or pesticides. Some plants have insect-repelling properties, while there are others whose leaves are turned into humus when they lose them in the fall. In addition to the chosen species, it is hoped that the scaffold will be spontaneously colonized by wild plants.

ARCHITECT
Édouard François

CLIENT
Paris Habitat

COLLABORATORS
Julien Odile (project manager),
Sophie Barbaux (landscaping), SICRA
(contractor)

TOTAL SURFACE AREA
83,000 sq ft

COST
USD 14,500,000

PROGRAM
Public housing project with
98 apartments and 11 artists' studios

Photography © David Boureau

The timber scaffold is anchored to the facade and provides most of the entrances, stairways, and communal areas. Its unique nature has turned the housing development into a landmark, even before being colonized by the plants.

Ground plan

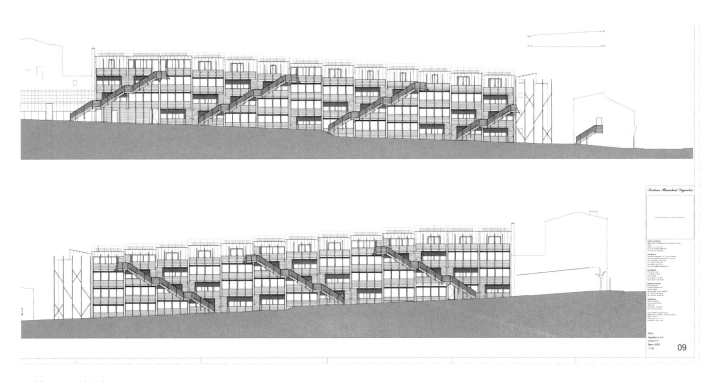

Buildings A and B elevations

There are two greenhouses in the complex built in
memory of the historic orchards that once covered
this district before urban sprawl and demographics
swallowed them up. They presently serve as a place for
the residents to collect their mail.

Building C elevation

Buildings S, T, and U elevations

The architect designed the project with the idea that
the dense timber trellises would become a leafy mass
of wisteria and other climbing vines and wild plant
species within five years.

MOSLER LOFTS

Seattle, WA, USA   2008

This 150-loft apartment building is located in the Belltown district of Seattle. The twelve-story building includes 6,000 sq ft of retail space and outdoor pedestrian spaces.

It is easily accessed on foot, and by bicycle, bus, and car. Residents are given membership to use the available hybrid cars. Despite the design favoring use of public transport, the building has an underground parking garage limited to just one car per apartment. Communal areas, such as shared living spaces, a rooftop garden, library, art gallery, business center, and three underground parking levels, as well as a community blog, help to create a community experience.

The building has a concrete and steel frame. The north roof area tilts to the south to maximize the efficiency of a future photovoltaic array.

60% of spaces receive natural light, while 55% of the building has natural ventilation. 43% of the exterior space at street level is landscaped with low-maintenance vegetation, and gardens occupy 18% of the roof. Other remarkable environmental aspects are hand-operable openings, roofs that provide shade, a system of interior sunshades, and setback glassing. These contribute to reducing the building's thermal load.

The property development company has invested in a program to offset 35% of the building's electrical use for two years.

ARCHITECT
Mithun

CLIENT
The Schuster Group

COLLABORATORS
Sider + Byers (mechanical engineering), JE Dunn NW, Kenneth Philp, Cary Kopczynski & Co, Holaday—Parks, Inc., Veca Electric, Hamasaki Consulting, Engineering Services, Bush Roed & Hitchings, SSA Acoustics, Atmosphere, Belltown Development Partners

TOTAL SURFACE AREA
243,000 sq ft (includes underground parking)

COST
USD 40,000,000

ENERGY REQUERIMENTS
3.84 kWh/sq ft/year

CERTIFICATION
USGBC LEED silver

PROGRAM
Mixed-use complex (residential and retail)

Photography © Benjamin Benschneider, Juan Fernández

Other environmental aspects are efficient windows, natural lighting, cross-ventilation, minimum finishes, and VOC-free materials, the use of recycled and reused materials, and reduction in water use.

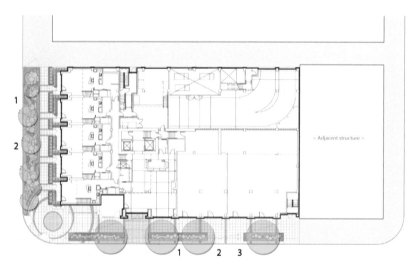

1) Water Effiecient Landscaping
2) "Green Street" Development
3) Public Transportation at Street

Site plan

1. Space for photovoltaic panels
2. Natural lighting
3. High-efficiency curtain walls and glazing
4. Water-conserving fixtures
5. Locally sourced material use
6. High-efficiency HVAC system
7. High-efficiency elevator system
8. High-efficiency boiler
9. Landscaped rooftop recreation areas
10. Green roof
11. Energy Star appliances
12. Certified wood
13. Enhanced Commissioning Systems
14. Underground parking
15. Hybrid car for members
16. Bicycle storage
17. Rainwater management
18. CO_2 monitoring
19. Selective waste collection
20. Evapotranspiration
21. Water infiltration

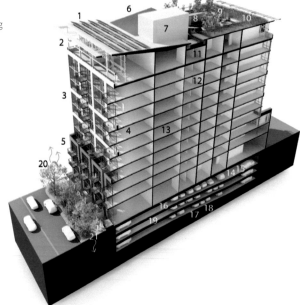

Section with environmental features

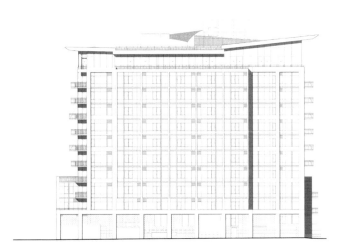

Northeast

Northeast elevation

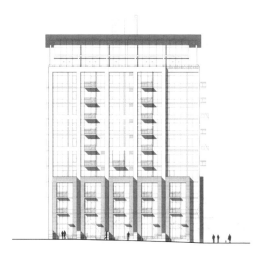

Northwest

Northwest elevation

Southwest

Southwest elevation

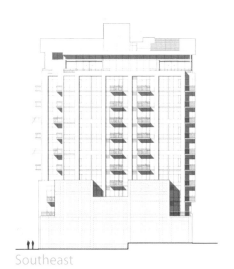

Southeast

Southeast elevation

All of the units are open-plan lofts with 10-ft high concrete ceilings, exposed ducts, wood floors, and floor-to-ceiling windows. Windows achieve Energy Star ratings, with low emissivity coatings and argon gas infill.

306

Level 5

Level 4

Level 3

Level 2

AIGUABLAVA HOUSING

Barcelona, Spain   2006

The first stage in the remodeling of Barcelona's Trinitat Nova district began in 2006, with the aim of building 189 homes. The area under transformation was characterized by a random layout of obsolete apartment blocks, with residual public spaces and hilly terrain. The planned development proposed a system of terraces that enabled the sloping site, crossed by the subway network, to be effectively developed, with the terraces serving as a base for the buildings.

Being a public housing project, this complex was pioneering in the use of elements for energy-saving and reconversion. It was the first in a future ecodistrict and it became the winner of the Premi Habitatge Social 2007 award.

The complex consists of dual-aspect apartments with cross-ventilation; solar protection; terraces and sliding sunshades; a ventilated facade in solid areas; a solar collector network; separate rainwater drainage; a gray water recovery system; and facades featuring reusable materials, minimizing waste. The buildings are six to eight stories, and have two basement levels.

The complex is a pioneering initiative in a city like Barcelona, which, since this construction began, has also announced the construction of a new ecodistrict in Vallbona for this decade. It is a major move for a place like Valbona, where the typical works of sustainable architecture have been limited to a few specific buildings or mixed-use complexes such as Ecourban 22@ designed by William McDonough + Partners.

ARCHITECT
Manuel Ruisánchez/Ruisánchez Arquitectes

CLIENT
INCASOL

COLLABORATORS
A. Sala, J.F. García/Robert Brufau i Associats (structure), Eulàlia Aran (quantity surveyor), Leopoldo Varas Corral (quantity surveyor)

HABITABLE SURFACE AREA
298,000 sq ft

COST
USD 23,957,000

PROGRAM
First-stage remodeling of a district with a 189-unit public housing project

Photography © Teresa Llordes

The project was built in a hilly area on an asymmetrical site and featured a high-density design. The site is literally wedged in a space between the city's urban area and Mount Collserola.

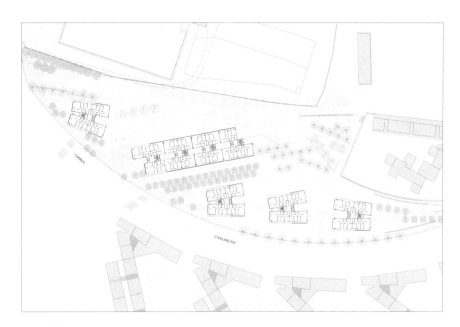

Ground plan

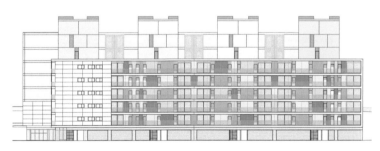

Front elevation

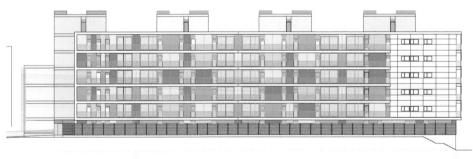

Rear elevation

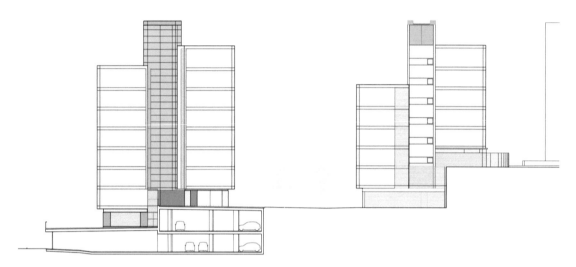

Side elevation

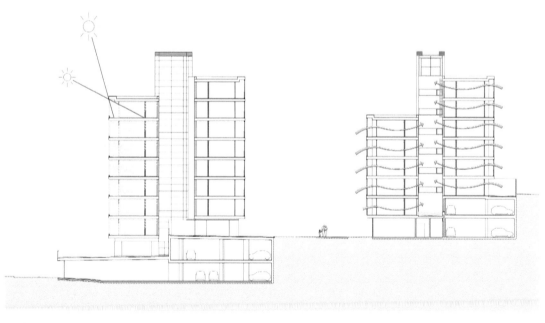

Bioclimatic sections

Owing to the long hours of sunlight in Barcelona, the facades feature sliding sunshades. When closed over the balconies, they create the impression of a series of enclosed galleries.

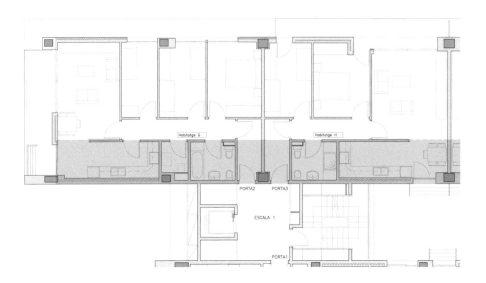

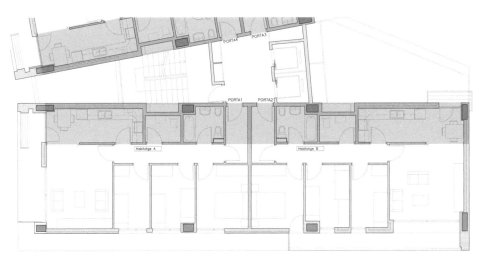

First floor and tower floor plan

RESIDENTIAL

3716 SPRINGFIELD

Kansas City, KS, USA   2009

Located in the Rosedale neighborhood, close to the University of Kansas Medical Center, this home is ideal for those who want to live "off the grid" without missing out on the amenities offered by living near the city's urban core.

Studio 804 is a nonprofit architectural practice that is part of the University of Kansas and aims to provide architectural solutions that respond to global problems related to density and sustainability, but from a local perspective. This studio, headed by Professor Dan Rockhill, has a radius of action focused on the areas of Kansas City and Lawrence, in the state of Kansas.

The program aimed for LEED platinum certification for the house, and to be the first home in Wyandotte County to use renewable energies. The upper level of the house contains four bedrooms, two bathrooms, and a toilet room. The master bedroom has a small terrace set back into the gable. The adjoining space, laid out as a loft, serves as an office or guest room, depending on the owners' needs at a given time. The open-plan downstairs area visually connects the kitchen, dining, and living room spaces.

The house is designed to produce surplus energy and sell it back to the grid. The roof features 600 sq ft of photovoltaic panels. These are complemented by a wind turbine and a geothermal energy source. The cellulose insulation in the walls and roof has a value of R-20.

The solid hardwood timber used on exterior walls was sourced from South America and is FSC certified. Interiors and the frame make use of seventy-year-old recycled Douglas fir.

ARCHITECT
Studio 804

CLIENT
Private

HABITABLE SURFACE AREA
2,500 sq ft

COST
USD 324,000

ENERGY CONSUMPTION
4.4 kWh/sq ft/year

CERTIFICATION
USGBC LEED platinum

PROGRAM
Single-family residence

Photography © Courtesy of Studio 804

The bedroom terrace is east facing. The west side of
the property borders a forested area that is not zoned
for future development.

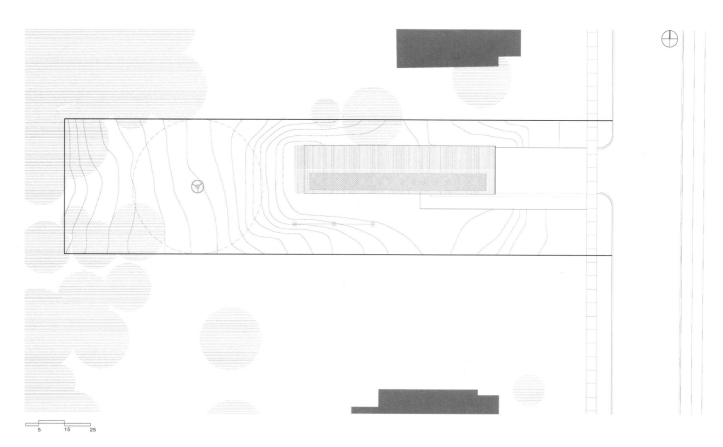

Site plan

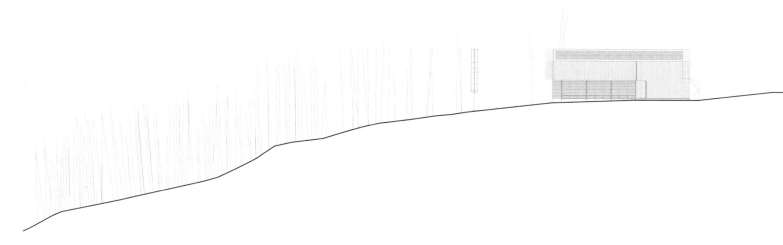

South elevation

The double-height space on the west and south sides
lets sunlight flood the interior. The heat is passively
retained overnight.

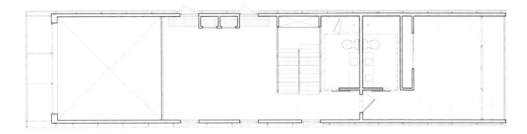

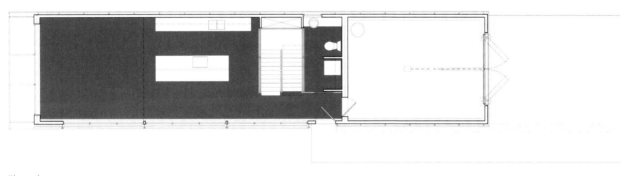

Floor plans

CLIFF HOUSE

Rosseau, Ontario, Canada   2008

This country house is located on a cliff overlooking a lake. To enhance its connection with its immediate surroundings, the architects made use of the local granite for the base of the building.

The clients wanted a retreat that would let them get away from it all and which had to be self-sufficient in its use of energy and water. The program was for a residence suitable for a family of four and included a kitchen, dining room, living area, library, and bedrooms. The house features a cantilevered roof and floor-to-ceiling windows on the facade facing the lake, adding lightness to the building and reinforcing the visual link between the living area and the body of water.

The design features strategies for passive solar gain, thermal mass, and good insulation to reduce the building's energy consumption. The overhanging roof areas prevent overheating in summer. The regulable windows at the core of the house enable use to be made of the solar chimney effect, in which hot air is expelled and replaced by cooler air. The green roof tempers the temperature changes between interior and exterior air and improves the integration of the house with the landscape.

In winter, the orientation of the windows toward the sun and glazed expanses, together with the thermal mass of the concrete floor slab and the stone walls, and the two complementary biomass heaters, cover the need for heating. The evacuated tube solar panels provide hot water for daily use, as well as for an additional floor heating system. The house also benefits from photovoltaic panels.

ARCHITECT
Altius Architecture

CLIENT
John and Cathy Phillips

COLLABORATORS
Trevor McIvor, Tony Round, CUCCO engineering + design, Doug Orchard/ Orchard Contracting

TOTAL SURFACE AREA
3,200 sq ft

COST
USD 1,930,980

PROGRAM
Single-family residence

Photography © Altius Architecture

Besides the regulating effect they exert on the
interior temperature, the green roofs also retain
water and provide a habitat for birds, insects, and
microorganisms.

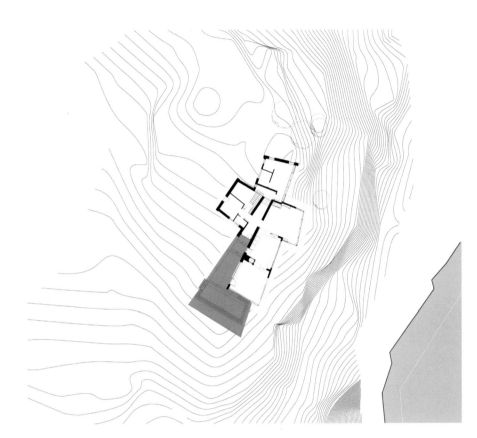

Site plan

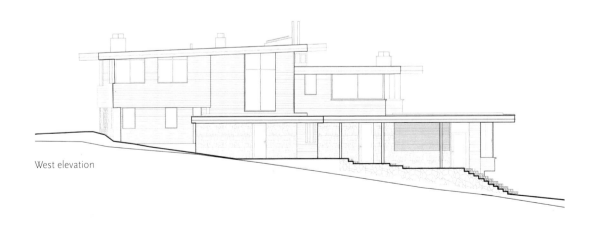

West elevation

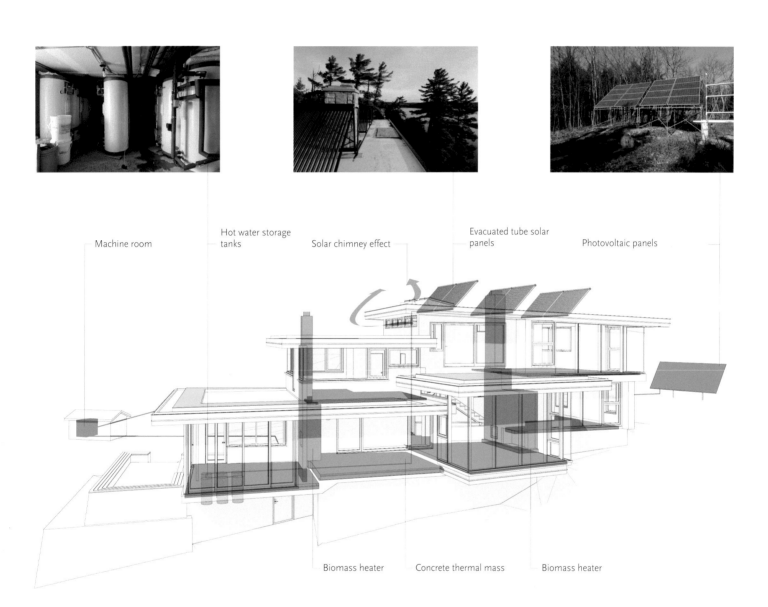

Machine room

Hot water storage
tanks

Solar chimney effect

Evacuated tube solar
panels

Photovoltaic panels

Biomass heater

Concrete thermal mass

Biomass heater

Diagram showing passive and active strategies

The house combines passive and active strategies
to satisfy its energy needs. Its staircase is located
centrally, and boosts the solar chimney effect to cool
interiors naturally.

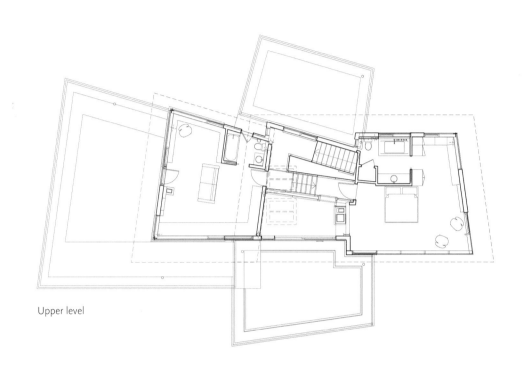

Upper level

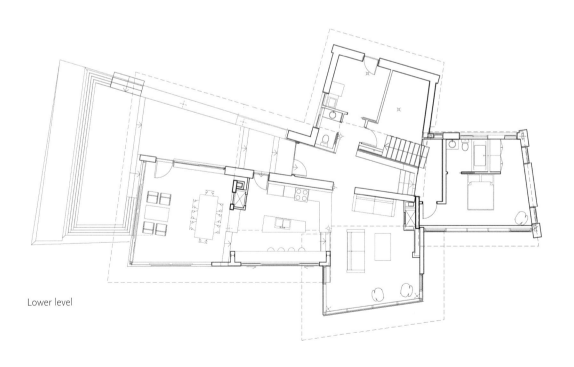

Lower level

THE GANANOQUE LAKE ROAD HOUSE

Gananoque, Ontario, Canada   2006

This basementless two-story home is located in Gananoque, a town of some fifty-three hundred inhabitants, and overlooks a large rural property in eastern Ontario.

Most of the rooms face south, which enables it to receive maximum solar passive heat gain in winter. The house is cool in summer, eliminating the need for air-conditioning, and features a heat-recovery ventilation system. A wood-burning stove also provides backup heat in winter.

The reinforced concrete structure was built using Durisol blocks, which contain recycled material. The concrete slab floor acts as a thermal mass, absorbing and releasing heat to regulate temperature changes.

The outside of the structure was sprayed with a 3-in thick layer of polyurethane foam as an insulating barrier. Ac-cording to the architect, this material is used instead of more natural alternatives like wool or recycled cellulose because the house required water-resistant insulation. The insulation on the exterior cladding enables the thermal mass inside the building to be maintained, which also helps to regulate the interior air temperature.

The windows and doors are low emissivity, triple-pane units with insulated fiberglass frames. The walls and roof are clad in Galvalume, low-maintenance steel that minimizes unwanted solar heat gain.

Water is heated by solar thermal panels. It is sourced from a well 300 ft away, and is used for domestic use and for the geothermal pump. The pump circulates the water to an aquifer, first moving it through the radiant underfloor system of the house.

ARCHITECT
Solares Architecture, Inc.

CLIENT
Brenda and James Lolley

HABITABLE SURFACE AREA
3,800 sq ft

COST
USD 630,000

ENERGY CONSUMPTION
8.2 kwh/sq ft/year

PROGRAM
Single-family residence

Photography © Solares Architecture, Inc.

One of the aims of the project was to create a highly energy-efficient skin. The interior is kept at a constant temperature during the day, eliminating the need for air-conditioning in summer and drastically reducing the need for heating in winter.

Perspective view of the north facade

Perspective view of the south facade

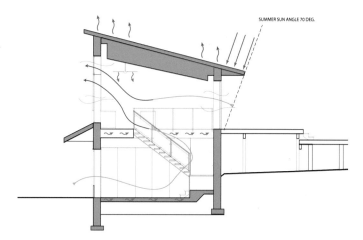

Bioclimatic diagram (summer)

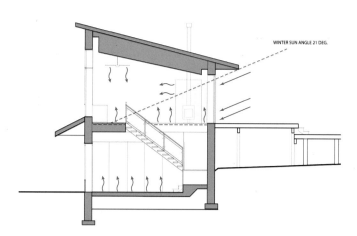

Bioclimatic diagram (winter)

The interiors feature healthy, nontoxic materials, with low-VOC paints. The kitchen and bathroom cabinets are formaldehyde free. The wood on stairs, window frames, skirting boards, and interior doors is locally sourced.

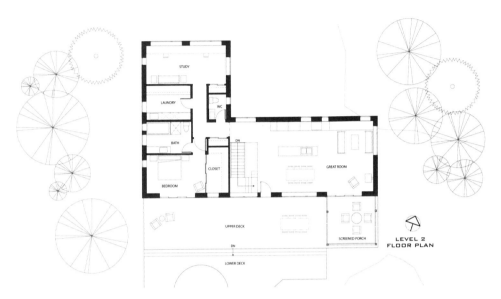

Upper level

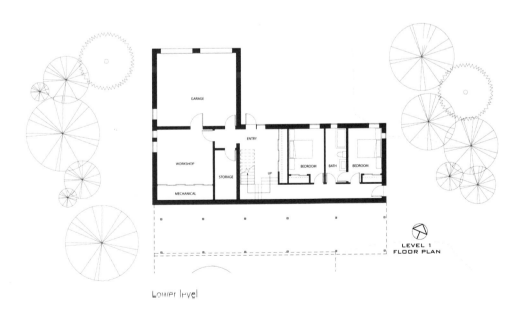

Lower level

FUJY PROJECT

El Escorial, Spain   2005

The fruit of participation from various universities, public entities, and companies, this project is currently being used as a prototype home for lectures and exhibitions of products related to sustainable architecture.

Each exterior wall has been designed to take advantage of weather conditions, depending on the season: air flow is used to cool in the summer, while the sun's rays are used to warm the house in the winter. The south-facing facade also features a number of systems to guarantee minimum energy consumption: aluminum louvers, thermal break joinery, greenhouses on the upper level, a solar dryer on the first floor, automatic security blinds, and special glazing to control thermal bridging.

Energy is supplied by passive systems (greenhouses, louvers, electric control vents, and overhanging roof areas) or active systems (solar thermal panels) together with supplementary backup from a high-performance boiler. There is also radiant floor heating-cooling and a gas water cooler.

Individual wireless thermostats regulate the temperature in each room. The roof is fitted with ecological insulation systems, a prefinished insulating frame (garage), slate tiling, and automatic ventilation windows to control the natural convection in the greenhouses. Thermal solar panels are also placed there to produce hot water for bathrooms and heating.

Rainwater is collected in an underground tank and is used for flushing toilets and washing clothes. All gray water and backwater produced in the home passes through a biological treatment plant and is reused for watering outdoor areas.

ARCHITECT
Luca Lancini/Fujy

CLIENT
Showroom house; no client

TOTAL SURFACE AREA
3,650 sq ft

PROGRAM
Single-family residence

Photography © Miguel de Guzmán

The outside walls are made from insulating brick
and panels of recycled gypsum board. A single-layer
waterproof finish has been applied to the outside walls
to raise the level of insulation.

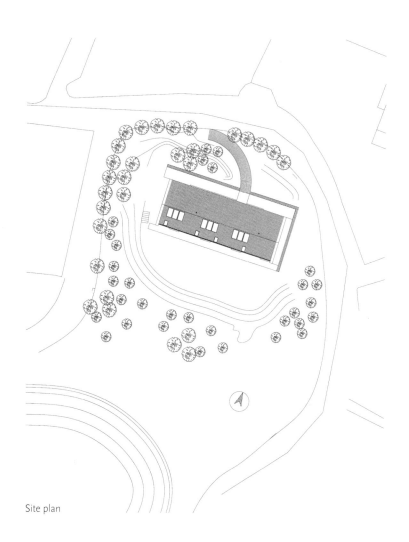

Site plan

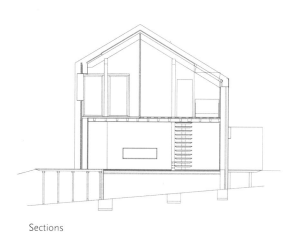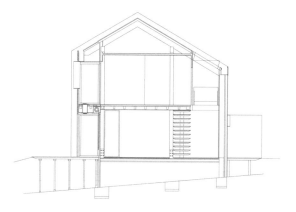

Sections

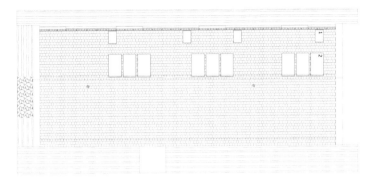

Roof plan

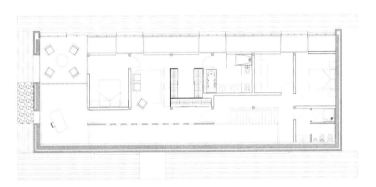

Upper level

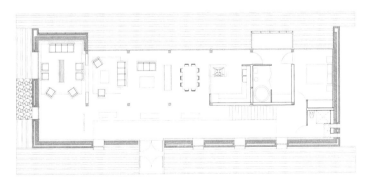

Lower level

The skylights installed in the gabled roof guarantee good interior lighting, particularly for areas with few windows.

SOLAR HOUSE III

Ebnat-Kappel, Switzerland   2000

Solar House III was built as a low-cost, zero-energy house. It includes a garage, plant room, and a basement. The structural frame is made from prefabricated wood, which enabled the house to be built in four months.

The house received the 2001 Prix Solaire Swiss award for its 474 sq ft south-facing solar wall, specially designed and built by the architect. Its energy panels contain paraffin, which melts and freezes according to the heat exchange between the interior and exterior temperature. The system is designed for the paraffin to have a thermal mass ten times greater than concrete in its natural state. The thin solar panel layers prevent overheating. This type of facade was first tested on this building, and technical advice was given by the Swiss Federal Office of Energy.

This facade is considered interactive. It operates according to the passive solar energy it receives to achieve a "transparent insulation" system. The insulated panels are made up of different low emissivity material layers. This system enables a balance to be achieved between solar gain and thermal loss.

There is total reflection of direct radiation from the house in summer, while lower-angled rays of winter sun can pass through this layer without any problem.

The photovoltaic panels can accumulate up to 2,500 kWh/year, far exceeding the building's 1,000 kWh/year thermal requirements.

ARCHITECT
Dietrich Schwarz

CLIENT
Suter and Truninger

COST
USD 509,000

CERTIFICATION
PassivHaus, Nullenergiehaus

PROGRAM
Single-family residence

Photography © Frédérik Comtesse

The spaces have an open feel produced by the
openings and convey simplicity and warmth through
the use of timber in the frame, ceilings, and floors.

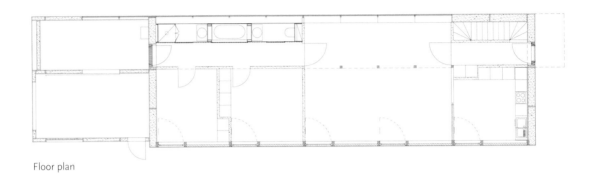

Floor plan

A simple succession of frosted glass panels separates
the passageway from the rooms. Even private spaces
such as the bathroom have large glazed expanses to
guarantee as much natural lighting as possible.

GREGÓIRE-OPDEBEECK HOUSE

Schaerbeek, Belgium
2003 (bulk of project) and 2008 (solar collector installation)

This home is a remodeling project of an old industrial laundry and includes low-energy consumption for compliance with the Swiss Minergie standard. The residence features a bioclimatic design with cross-ventilation through the central skylights in the living area. The environmental goal in the remodeling of the building was to meet energy requirements with 60% of power derived from solar energy, 20% from biomass, and 20% from gas. The building complies with the Belgian low-energy consumption standard for the Brussels region, with 5.5 kWh/ sq ft/year to cover heating needs.

Energy use prior to the remodeling was 20.4 kWh/sq ft/year, so the reduction achieved is in the region of 63%. Residual heat and the production of hot water for daily use is 75% ensured by the installation of 172 sq ft of evacuated solar thermal panels and a biomass (wood) heater. The remaining 25% is provided by a condensing boiler using biomethane.

Electrical energy is produced by fourteen high-performance photovoltaic panels (440 sq ft) supplying 75% of the domestic power requirements. The other 25% is purchased from a renewable energy supplier. The investment in renewable energy technology is planned to be recouped in six or seven years. A 5,300 gallon rainwater tank supplies needs for nondrinking water.

The four-bedroom residence has a rectangular floor plan. The upper level is clad in wooden slats. The lower level floor slab is paved with ceramic tiles.

ARCHITECT
Marc Opdebeeck

CLIENT
Gregóire Opdebeeck

TOTAL SURFACE AREA
2,045 sq ft

ENERGY CONSUMPTION
8 kWh/sq ft/year

CERTIFICATION
Minergie

PROGRAM
Single-family residence remodeling

Photography © Marie-Hélène Grégoire, Jacky Delorme

The house is clad in wooden slats with a zinc roof.
Mineral wool insulation is used on exterior walls
and in the roof. Interiors are insulated with 3 in thick
mineral wool batts without air chambers.

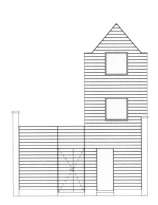 

Front and rear elevations

Cross-section

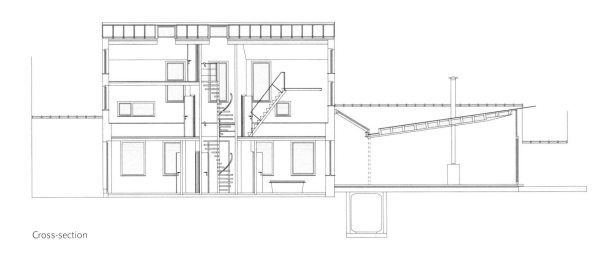

Cross-section

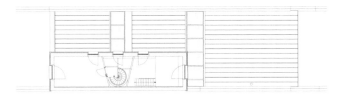

Third floor

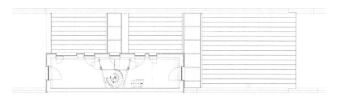

Second floor

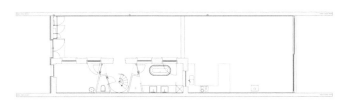

First floor

VILLA WELPELOO

Enschede, Netherlands   2009

2012Architecten is a Rotterdam practice that was set up in 1997 and specializes in research and experimentation with the material cycle for self-build. What is considered by some to be waste material is used by this practice to enhance the flow of materials and energy. Their supply of raw material is local, given that they normally recover materials they find near the building site.

The practice is the result of a study on the environmental impact and cost of reusing materials to build a house. The study analyzed greenhouse gas emissions, energy use, and carbon imprint for the entire recycling process. The environmental impact of reused materials, such as wood facades and steel frames were also analyzed. Then results were compared with the cost and impact of the same amount of material if all of it were new instead of recycled and repurposed.

From an environmental perspective, the outcome was clearly in favor of reused material. However, the experimental nature of the reutilized material meant that the costs of the project were higher than they would be if conventional building materials were used.

Repurposing waste materials allows for the redesign of conventional forms and building techniques. The building's structural frame is made from steel sourced from an old textile factory, the remnants of a sector that was once thriving in the Netherlands. One of the machines recovered from the textile factory was enough to provide all of the steel used in the residence. The house's timber planks are from cable reels, are of a standard size, and are in good condition. These planks, removed from a thousand cable reels from the TKF Company, were enough to clad the facade.

ARCHITECT
2012Architecten

CLIENT
Private

COLLABORATORS
Plato International BV Arnhem (timber), Houtwerk Delft (custom closets), Smile Plastics, UK (bathroom tiles), Marike Den Haag (sanitary fixtures), Atelier En-fer (lighting structure), Jansen Janisol (joinery)

TOTAL SURFACE AREA
2,700 sq ft

COST
USD 1,220,000

ENERGY CONSUMPTION
12.2 kWh/sq ft/year

PROGRAM
Single-family residence with 60% recycled materials

Photography © Allard van der Hoek

The facade is clad with planks from cable reels
sourced from a local cable manufacturer. 1,000 cable
reels were needed for the exterior and for internal
partitions.

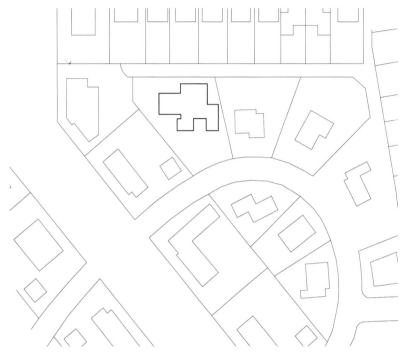

Site plan

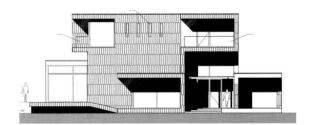 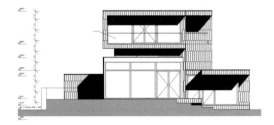

Elevations

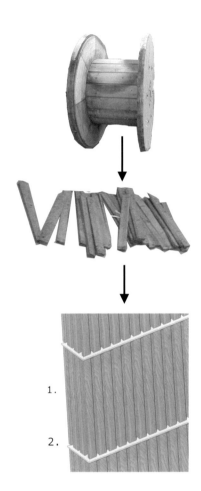

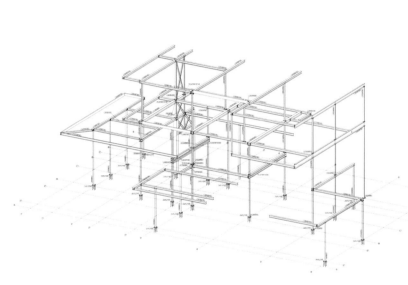

Diagram showing the steel frame

Diagram showing the origin of the timber planks

The project was for a couple with an art collection. The design included two bedrooms, a combined kitchen and study, an open-plan living area at the core of the house, and a guest room.

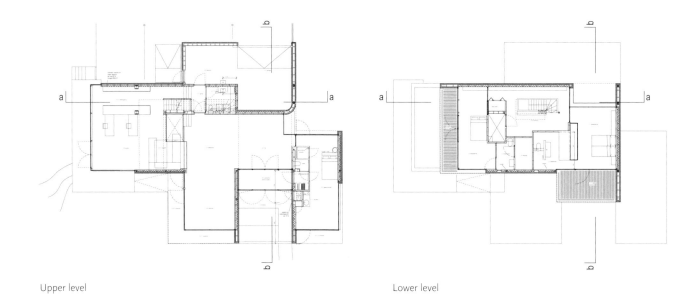

Upper level

Lower level

SENSIBLE HOUSE

Douglas County, KS, USA   2008

The architects describe this house as being very visible from a distance, owing to its white walls and roof, which convey a feeling of purity in the midst of a vast landscape.

The program consisted of creating a comfortable and contemporary home in a predominantly rural area. The home is well oriented, made from natural materials, and has low heating and maintenance requirements.

There is a three-car garage at the entrance to the property and space for a future orchard and garden. The house has three bedrooms, each with an en suite bathroom. The open plan means that the living areas are connected to the kitchen and bedrooms. The master bedroom and dining area open onto a 400 sq ft courtyard.

The common area is in the south wing and consists of a plant room, guest bathroom, and storm shelter, in case of tornados. The large open kitchen has Swedish furnishings and a countertop partly made of recycled paper. Storage space is provided by floor-to-ceiling closets.

External walls are clad in recycled steel panels. A central vacuum system keeps inside air healthy, and radiant floor heating has been installed for warmth. The south-facing building maximizes passive solar gain and improves the quality of the living space. If the bioclimatic design does not provide sufficient air flow, there are also two air-conditioning systems in the house for use in summer.

ARCHITECT
Rockhill + Associates

CLIENT
Private

HABITABLE SURFACE AREA
2,400 sq ft

COST
USD 459,000

ENERGY CONSUMPTION
11 kWh/sq ft/year

PROGRAM
Single-family residence

Photography © Dan Rockhill

The clients' requirements included making the house
free of volatile organic compounds like formaldehyde
in its finishings, and making its rooms wheelchair
accessible.

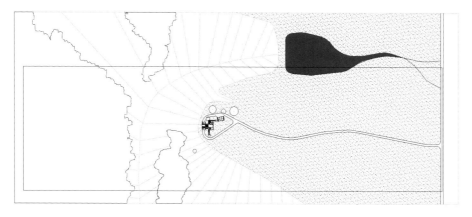

Site plan

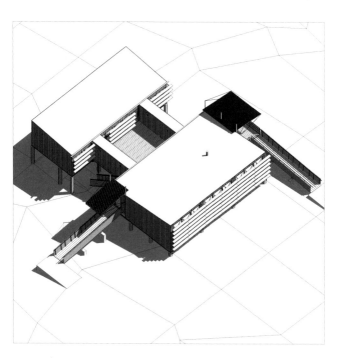

3-D aerial view

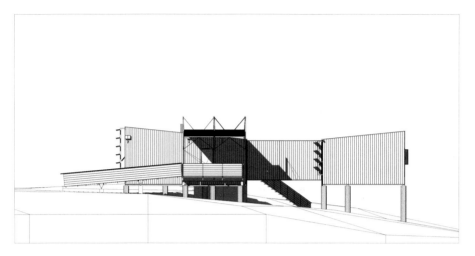

East elevation

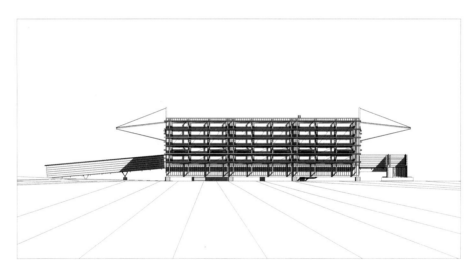

South elevation

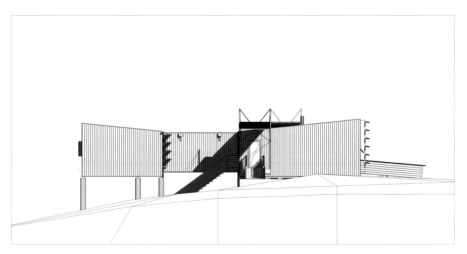

West elevation

The south facade enhances passive solar gain with its glazed expanse. Regulable louvers offer protection from overheating in especially sunny conditions.

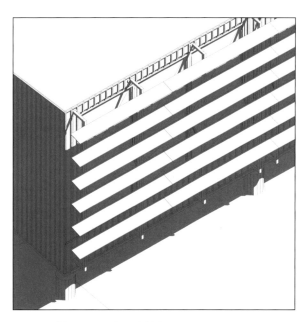

3-D view of the system of regulable louvers

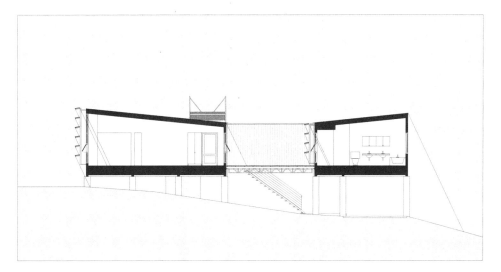

Bioclimatic section (summer)

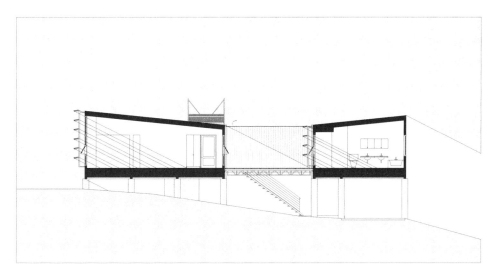

Bioclimatic section (winter)

HANSSEN-HÖPPENER HOUSE

Selfkant-Großwehrhagen, Germany   2007

Ludwig Rongen, architect and urban planner, is specialized in building passive houses with a close to zero net-energy balance. This single-family home he engineered is located in a mainly rural setting. The program responded to the needs of a Dutch couple who wanted a decidedly ecofriendly dwelling with good interior air quality.

Most of the main rooms are south facing. The lower level houses the living area, a bathroom, the open-plan kitchen, pantry or storeroom, transit areas, and plant room. The upper level contains the bedrooms, study, another bathroom, dressing room, and a double-height space that serves as a gallery and solar collector.

This is a zero-emissions house that generates more energy than it needs. Heating and power is provided by a biomass furnace and photovoltaic array producing 3.0 kW per panel. There is also a heat-cold pump used to cool the house in summer. The main frontage is clad in larch wood and finished in a fine colored film that is permeable to ambient humidity.

Hot water for daily use is stored in a water heater. The lower-floor walls are glazed from east to west, although the first floor overhangs to offer protection for the west, east, and, south facades. There are barely any openings on the north facade.

ARCHITECT
Rongen Architekten

CLIENT
Climmy Hanssen and François Höppener

COLLABORATORS
Friedhelm Lindgens, Reiner Wirtz

TOTAL SURFACE AREA
2,200 sq ft

COST
USD 488,000

ENERGY CONSUMPTION
1.2 kWh/sq ft/year

CERTIFICATION
PassivHaus

PROGRAM
Single-family residence

Photography © Rongen Architekten

Passive houses normally stand out for their sparse designs. Rongen has created a geometric volume, with larch wood on the southern facade and partially on the east and west sides, of the upper-level cladding.

Site plan

Elevations

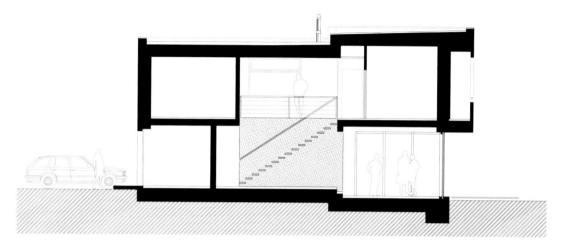

Longitudinal section

The open-plan kitchen and living-dining areas are laid
out in a double-height void filled with natural light
entering from the glass expanse on the facade of the
lower level and the picture window upstairs.

Upper level

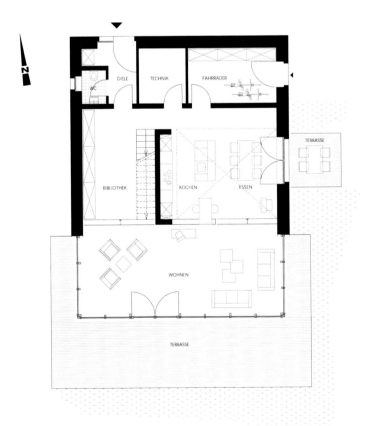

Lower level

OFF-THE-GRID RESIDENCE

Murphys, CA, USA   2009

This house was designed as a summer and winter house for a San Francisco couple and their two young children. It is not connected to a sewerage network or an electricity grid. The space is divided into public and private areas, each with 1,600 sq ft of floor space, laid out to afford views of the California Gold Country, a few miles away from the small town of Murphys.

The gaps between the two buildings under the overhangs are to funnel breezes coming from the valley. The courtyard is a quiet space for relaxation and a play area for the children.

The environmental features of the buildings were agreed upon with the client, who is a real estate developer. They comprise: large overhangs to maximize shade in summer and allow passive solar gain in winter; low-emissivity glass in windows and skylights, all regulable to improve cross-ventilation—they open at night to enable the cool to eliminate heated air from the interior, and they are closed during the day; facades and a roof made from structural insulated panels (SIPs); large north-facing windows for maximum sunlight; overhangs and arbor roofs have foil backing to reflect summer heat; and a solar chimney effect to remove hot air from the interiors.

The house has an array of photovoltaic panels with battery storage. The estimated energy demand is 3 kWh, its energy system provides 3.3 kWh.

ARCHITECT
Cass Smith/Cass Calder Smith Architecture

CLIENT
Private

COLLABORATORS
Kleinfelder (geotechnics), Geddings Engineering (structural engineering), Sol Sierra Solar Energy Systems (energy consultants), Sonoma Mission Gardens (landscaping)

TOTAL SURFACE AREA
3,200 sq ft

COST
USD 350,000

ENERGY CONSUMPTION
0.002 kWh/sq ft/year

PROGRAM
Single-family residence

Photography © Brendan P Macrae, Prime Lens Photography

The house has twenty-four photovoltaic panels with battery storage and a backup propane generator. Water is from a well pumped by photovoltaic energy to a storage tank.

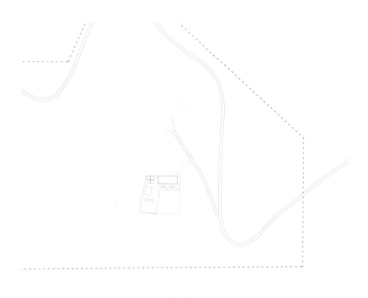

Site plan

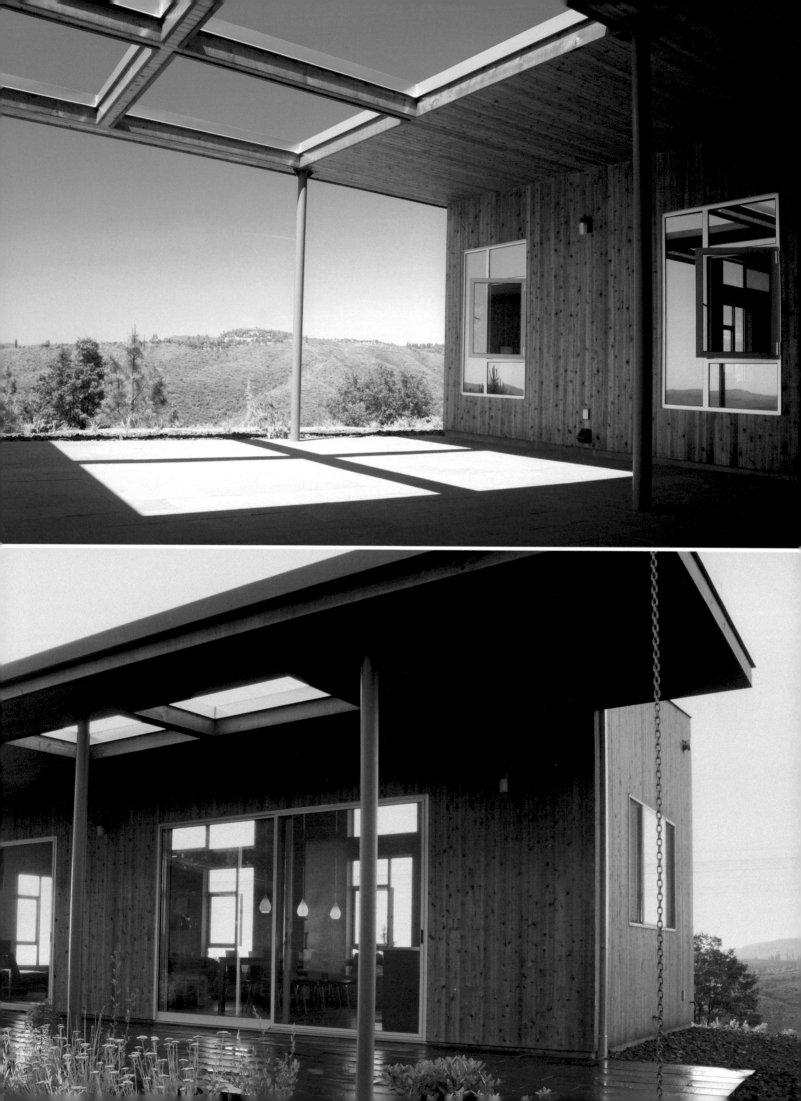

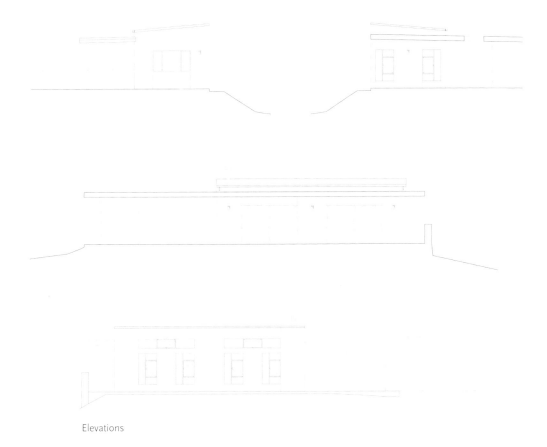

Elevations

Radiant floor heating is fed by a propane boiler and
a high-efficiency biomass stove in the living area.
Low-VOC paints were used, and the floor is polished
concrete.

LIVE BUILDING
SLEEP BUILDING

1. Courtyard
2. Breezeway
3. Lookout
4. Kitchen
5. Dining area
6. Living area
7. Transit area
8. Bedrooms
9. Bathrooms

Ground plan

FLEG DAIKANYAMA

Tokyo, Japan   2005

The site is located between a residential area and a business district. These areas are connected by an alley.

The building consists of a concrete structure with an asymmetrical floor plan comprising three above-ground floors and one basement level. The underground level houses five retail spaces.

The building is squeezed between two white concrete walls located south and north of the central volume. These serve to define a common area between the two ends of the building. The space between both dividing walls at the height of the second floor features a series of beams planted with hydroponically grown moss. According to the ar-chitect, this green contrast in a building dominated by light colors is a visual and playful re-creation of vegetation—quite symbolic in a city as densely populated and polluted as Tokyo.

When the climate is too dry, the moss withdraws, showing its darker side and the absence of life. When it rains, the moss sprouts and turns the galvanized steel beams into bright green expanses.

The roof of the building is a terrace featuring a cube-like structure housing the plant room. The project is more symbolic than ecological; it does, however, serve to transmit the importance of greenery to the building's tenants, in a city as built up as the Japanese capital.

ARCHITECT
Taketo Shimohigoshi/A. A. E.

CLIENT
FLEG International Co., Ltd.

COLLABORATORS
G.DeSIGN, ES Associates, Total Environmental Engineers

TOTAL SURFACE AREA
8,277 sq ft

COST
USD 2,173,500

PROGRAM
Office and retail space

Photography © Shigeo Ogawa, Koichi Torimura

Hydroponics is the method used to grow plants using mineral solutions instead of soil. This technology enables surfaces to be covered with vegetation when they are not suitable for planting with soil.

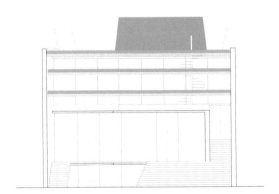

Elevations

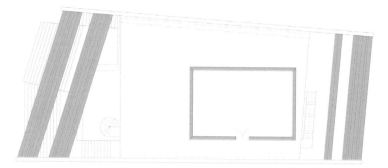

Roof plan

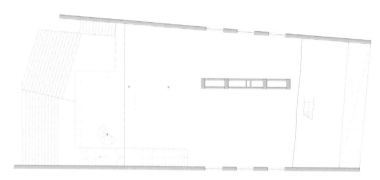

Second floor

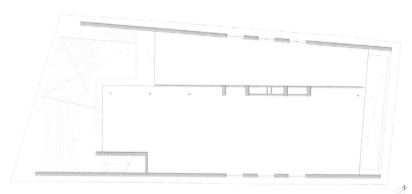

First floor

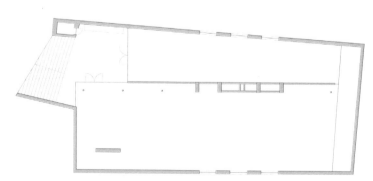

Basement

The cube on the roof terrace features a vertical garden
grown hydroponically.

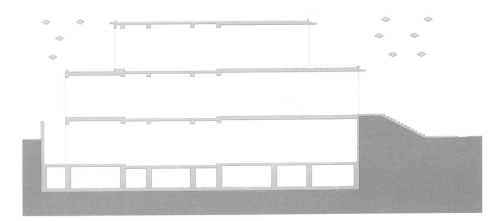

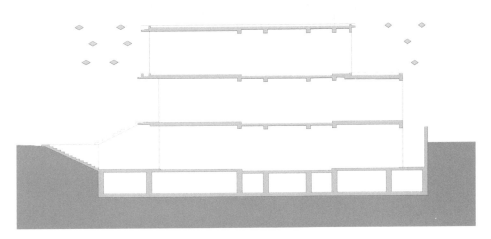

Sections

PREFABRICATED

"DRAGEN" CHILDREN'S HOUSE

Odense, Denmark   2009

This building combines sustainability criteria with a design that enhances its educational features. The purpose of the design was to raise the comfort level for the children and the sense of well-being offered by the day care center.

The building is laid out over two levels, with the children's area on the south side. The two levels are connected by stairwells and ramps, designed with the children's sensory and motor development in mind.

A total of 4,500 sq ft of play space was created for the eighty-eight children (forty-four babies and forty-four children under school age); standards normally apply a minimum of 2,900 sq ft. This leaves more space for activities and when combined with the use of natural materials, reduces the incidence of illness being spread from child to child.

The building is perfectly insulated, which means energy savings of 20% compared to a conventional building. It is made from prefabricated wood panels with wide glazed expanses on facades that let in abundant natural light and take advantage of passive solar gain. This is complemented by solar thermal and photovoltaic panels and a heat-recovery ventilation system.

A touch screen in the foyer of the building informs parents of the building's energy performance at all times. The internal comfort conditions are guaranteed by the use of materials certified by Nordic Swan. This standard certifies the natural origin of these materials, from their raw state to their final product.

ARCHITECT
C. F. Møller Architects

CLIENT
Odense City Council

COLLABORATORS
Tækker Rådgivende Ingeniører (engineering), C. F. Møller Architects (landscaping)

TOTAL SURFACE AREA
11,000 sq ft

COST
USD 3,255,000

ENERGY CONSUMPTION
1.4 kWh/sq ft/year

CERTIFICATIONS
Passivhaus, Nordic Swan

PROGRAM
Day care center for 88 children and 14 caregivers

Photography © Uffe Johansen

Low energy use is achieved by means of insulation and control of the ventilation and heat-recovery system. When the inside temperature rises because of the children's activity, the ventilation system works overtime to extract excess heat from the rooms.

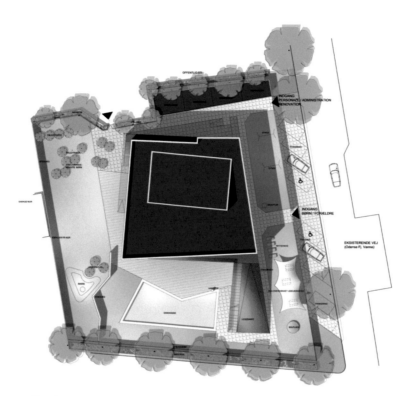

Site plan

5

6

1. Cool air intake / inside air extraction
2. Tempered cool air
3. Hot inside air
4. Insulation
5. Compact form
6. Orientation

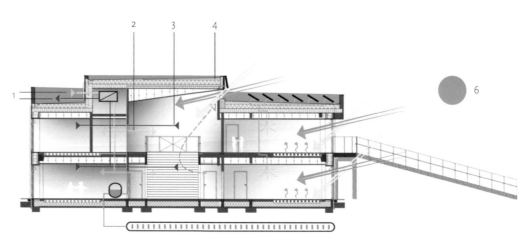

Passive air-conditioning and heat-recovery ventilation system

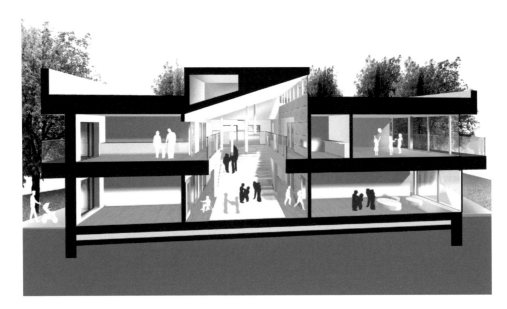

3-D section

Upper level

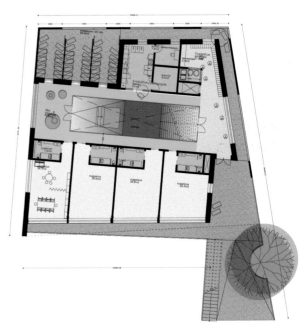

Lower level

CAMP WILDALPEN MOUNTAIN RESORT

Wildalpen, Austria   2006

Located in a rural setting near the Salza River, this resort was financed by the European Union's Leader Plus project and the provincial government of Styria. This project has the goal of fostering the development of traditional, regional architecture. It complies with the unofficial Niedrigenergiehaus standard, which applies to low-energy buildings.

Holz Box won the 2003 design competition for the building of a multifunctional, modular resort. They had developed a similar project in Passail in 2004. The Wildalpen building, smaller than its predecessor, is an extension to the existing Wildwasserzentrum (whitewater center), which is a magnet for lovers of the mountains, backcountry skiing, kayaking, and rafting.

The building's rectangular structure is anchored to the ground by a series of columns. The lower level houses systems installations and a room to store maintenance materials. There is plenty of open space for parking or to be used as a meeting area.

A staircase connects the upper and lower levels of the building. It's main entrance, which is located on the upper level, leads to a foyer, one of the few communal areas in the building.

The structure is divided into five apartment modules and one module of the same size, which houses the communal area. Each module has a floor space of 377 sq ft and features a core area where its bathrooms and kitchen are located. Some of the furnishings, such as the bunk beds, are built in. Small bedrooms line the east and west facades. Their privacy is guarded with sliding doors.

ARCHITECT
Holz Box

CLIENT
Naturfreunde Österreich

COLLABORATORS
JR Consult (structural engineers)

TOTAL SURFACE AREA
2,600 sq ft

COST
USD 677,230

ENERGY CONSUMPTION
4.55 kWh/sq ft/year

PROGRAM
Mountain accommodation

Photography © Birgit Koell

The layout of interior spaces provides all of the
bedrooms with natural light. The apartment modules
have covered open areas on the east facade.

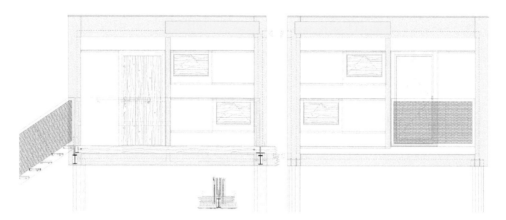

Apartment module cross-sections

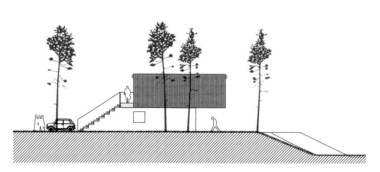

North elevation

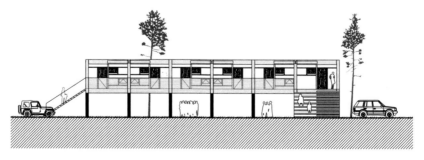

West elevation

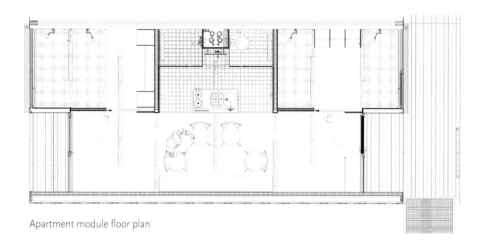

Apartment module floor plan

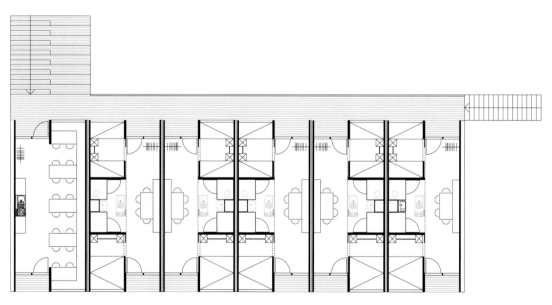

Upper level

SUSTAINABLE PROTOTYPE: ARTS CENTER

Greensburg, KS, USA   2008

Studio 804 is a nonprofit design and construction program run by the University of Kansas for graduating students in its Architecture and Urban Planning program. It focuses on prefabricated building systems and responds to the general problems of adapting building prototypes to suit local contexts.

The Sustainable Prototype was built and delivered a year after a tornado devastated the Greensburg area. The design responded to the specific brief of the 5.4.7 Arts Center, the principal client, and was intended to act as a community center for the area, a meeting point symbolizing the spirit and courage behind the area's rebuilding.

During the design of the studio, following the tornado, Greensburg City Council ordered that all publicly subsidized buildings to be rebuilt according to the U.S. Green Building Council's LEED platinum rating criteria. Although the Arts Center did not require public funding, Studio 804 chose to follow the guidelines of this rating system as an act of responsibility, and actually became the first building in Kansas to receive LEED platinum level certification.

According to the student team that designed it, the chief environmental positives of the prototype were its seamless blending with the landscape, strategic use of active and passive strategies to meet energy requirements (80%–120% depending on the season and wind speed), use of recycled materials, and flexibility for use as an exhibition space, community center, assembly hall, or space for offices.

It features wind turbines that supply an estimated 430 kWh/month of energy for a mean wind speed of 11 mph. Photovoltaic solar panels contribute 1.4 kWh.

ARCHITECT
Studio 804

CLIENT
5.4.7 Arts Center

TOTAL SURFACE AREA
1,680 sq ft

COST
USD 496,600

CERTIFICATION
USGBC LEED platinum

PROGRAM
Cultural facility

Photography © Courtesy of Studio 804

Greensburg is located in Kiowa County, in southwestern Kansas, a state with a large farming sector. In May 2007, the town was devastated by a tornado that destroyed 95% of its buildings and left eleven people dead.

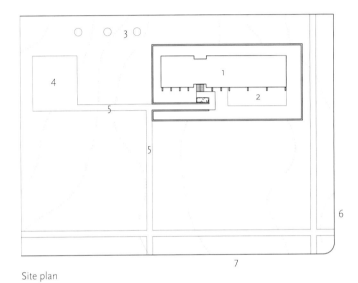

1. Sustainable prototype
2. Elevated platform
3. Wind turbine towers
4. Parking
5. Path leading to the ramp
6. Sycamore Street
7. Wisconsin Street

Site plan

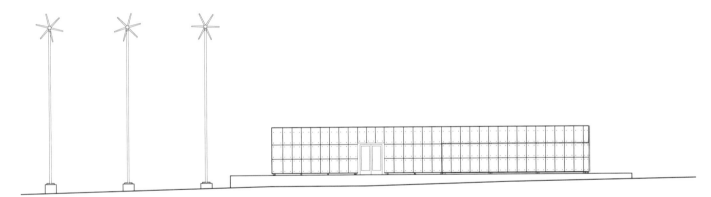

South Elevation

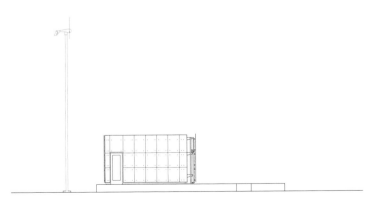

West Elevation

The students participated in the building of the prototype, assisted by specialized labor. Building time was ninety days. The building has a structural frame made from FSC-certified wood covered in a glass skin.

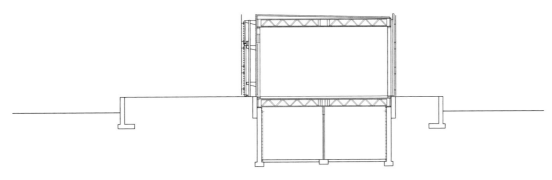

Cross-section

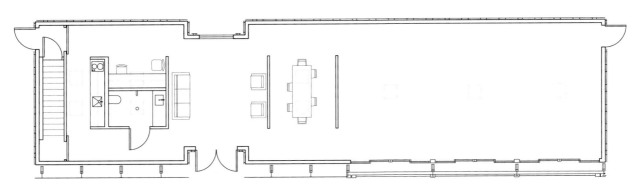

Floor plan

BARK STUDIO

Noosa Hinterland, Queensland, Australia   2001

This building is a steel and glass pavilion with strong modernist lines. It is flexible as a studio for five or six employees, but can also serve as a residence for two people.

The design began with a prefabricated volume, which can be transported to another location. Although the design required eighteen months, the erection of its prefabricated structure only needs between five and six days. In order to minimize costs and building time, standard modules were used for this building, with plywood for floors, ceilings, and walls.

The result is a building that rises harmoniously between two Australian bloodwood trees with a rectangular module measuring 66 ft in length. The outer walls are openable and there are fixed glazed expanses on three sides. The closed fourth facade faces the road and is a plywood box that provides privacy and protection from the western sun.

The environmental features of the project are: respect for its location; maximizing and regulating cross- and stack-effect ventilation; the use of light materials such as the plywood sourced from sustainable plantations; earthquake resistance; and the use of solar protections such as awnings and fabric curtains.

The lower level holds the main areas, including the kitchen, laundry, bathroom, storeroom, and space for vertical transit. The mezzanine has space for a library, sleeping area, and shower.

ARCHITECT
Bark Design Pty, Ltd.

CLIENT
Bark Design Pty, Ltd.

COLLABORATORS
Ron Scholes Building, Tod Noosa (structural engineering)

SURFACE AREA
1,100 sq ft

COST
USD 179,300

ENERGY CONSUMPTION
1 kWh/sq ft/year

PROGRAM
Architectural practice with place for overnight stay

Photography © Christopher Frederick Jones, Vincent Long

The rectangular volume offers maximum views of the Pacific coast. It expresses lightness, transparency, texture, seamless blending with the landscape, and a response to the climate.

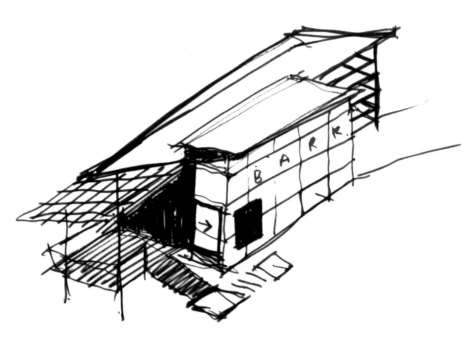

Rendering

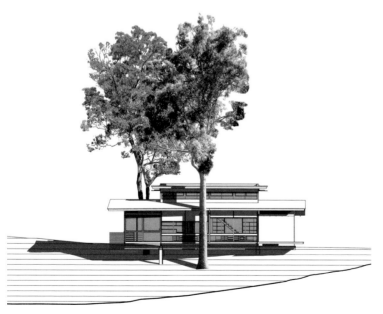

Northeast elevation

Southwest elevation

Room Key

8 - Reading
9 - Sleeping
10 - Bathroom

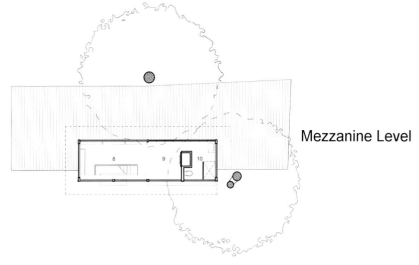

Mezzanine Level

Mezzanine

Room Key

1 - Deck
2 - Workspace
3 - Library
4 - Laundry/WC
5 - Kitchen
6 - Meeting Area
7 - Services

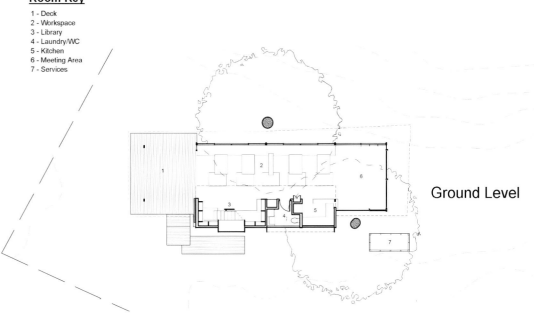

Ground Level

Lower level

INFINISKI MANIFESTO HOUSE

Curacaví, Chile   2009

This house stands on a hilltop. It was designed as a green architectural manifesto from 85% recycled, reused, and ecofriendly materials such as recycled galvanized steel or bay laurel wood, which was reused in the house's kitchen units and closets.

The house is laid out around a large enclosed central space on the north-south axis, creating volumetric stress toward one of the views, given that the east-west axis is permeable and offers magnificent opportunities to view sunrises and sunsets.

Modular construction of the building provided savings in transport and waste. The structure consists of three reused shipping containers. The two containers forming the upper level rest on one container divided into two parts, forming the lower level. This portico-like structure creates extra floor space between the containers, so that three containers with a combined floor space of 1,000 sq ft (each container is 333.33 sq ft) are able to create the total floor space of 1,700 sq ft.

The house dresses up and dresses down in summer and winter, respectively, by means of a transventilated skin on the facades and roofs. It dresses up by using the skin in summer to protect itself from the sun, creating a natural passive cooling effect. It dresses down in winter by removing the skin to enable the sun to create a natural passive heating effect by hitting the metal surface of the container and by entering the windows.

Sprayed cellulose from recycled newspapers is used on outer walls as insulation, while ecological cork is used as underfloor insulation. These passive thermal insulating elements are combined with alternative energy technology (solar thermal panels) to achieve 70% energy self-sufficiency.

ARCHITECT
James & Mau

CLIENT
Infiniski Sustainable Architecture and Construction

TOTAL SURFACE AREA
1,700 sq ft

COST
USD 107,150

PROGRAM
Single-family country house

Photography © Antonio Corcuera

Two kinds of skins are used on the facades: The first is made from fixed horizontal timber slats, and the second is made from moving pallets that can be opened individually to control solar radiation. The roof skin can be installed and removed according to the season.

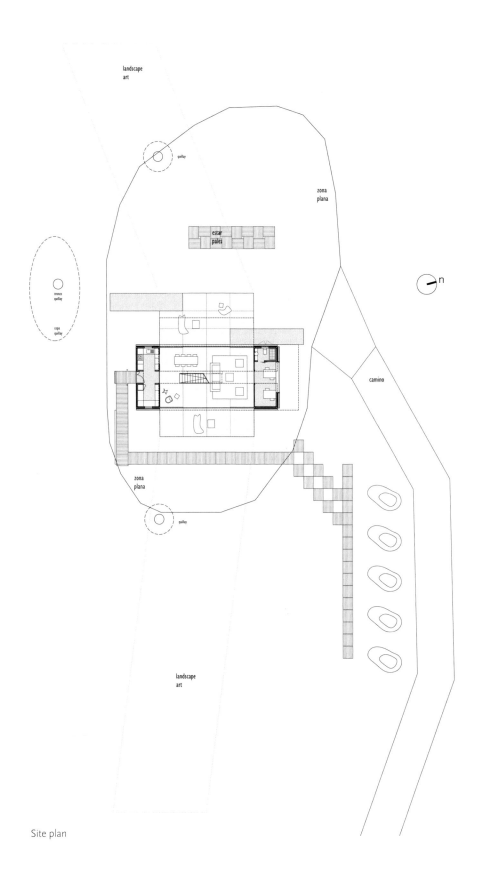

Site plan

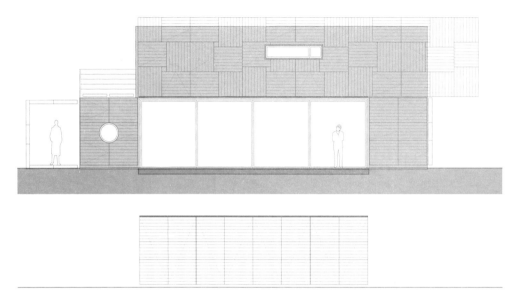

East elevation

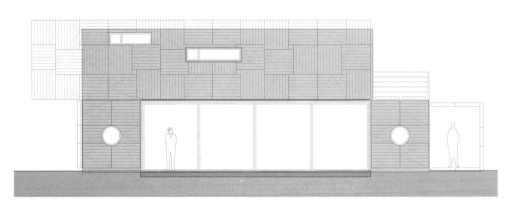

West elevation

The canopies are raised in winter to let the light from the low sun enter and create a greenhouse effect inside. They are lowered in summer in varying degrees, depending on the time of day and outside temperature, for a natural ventilation effect.

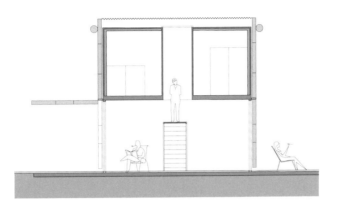

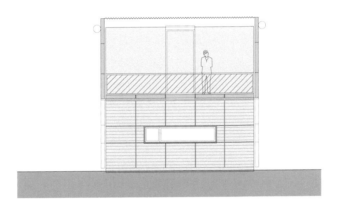

Cross-section and north elevation (rear)

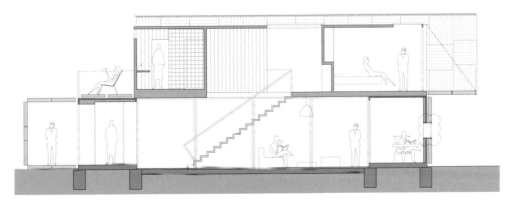

Longitudinal section

The dwelling is divided into two levels: a combined
living and dining room, a kitchen, bedroom,
bathroom, and patios on the lower floor; and the
master bedroom and en suite bathroom, a living area,
two bedrooms with a shared bathroom, and terraces
on the upper level.

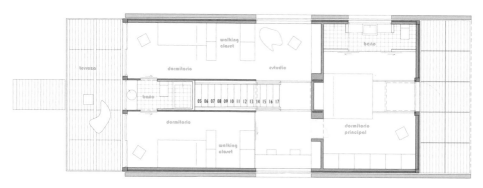

Upper level

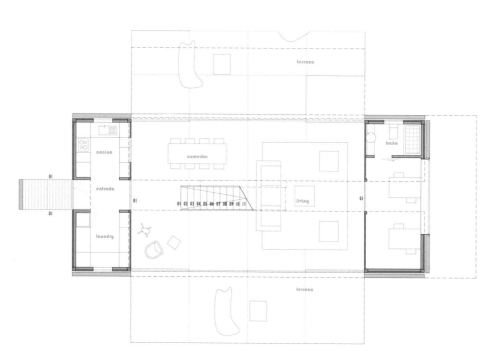

Lower level

THE QUIK HOUSE

Tewksbury, NJ, USA   2008

The Quik House, designed by Adam Kalkin at the beginning of the last decade, is the forerunner to this model, called the Old Lady House by its creator. The first Quik House prototype was built in New Jersey in 2002. The first full-scale model was built in 2006 in Kenvil, where the layout was refined. An even better prototype was later installed in Tewksbury.

The design is forward thinking, but the project has an industrial look. It was a house made from shipping containers, and it does not hide this particular feature. The floor plan does not allow for large spaces, so the existing ones respond strictly to function.

The containers are finished in a factory, with connections and services included. The foundation, however, is prepared on site. Its glass panes are installed on site and the connections are finished on site. After its assembly, the structure is sprayed with a fireproof membrane and the green roof is planted. It takes approximately three months to manufacture and assemble the structure.

The house is laid out with a kitchen, living and dining area, laundry and toilet on the lower level, where the flooring is radiant, and three bedrooms and two bathrooms upstairs. Another container facing the house serves as an extension building with a lower level for storage and an upper level for guests, with a bathroom, two libraries, a reading room, a closet, and an open central space for children to play in or for receiving guests. The two upper levels are joined by a balcony-bridge on the south facade.

ARCHITECT
Adam Kalkin/Quik Build

CLIENT
Jorge Hribaty

COLLABORATORS
Andy Johnston, George Cooper, Jeff Bravestein

HABITABLE SURFACE AREA
2,000 sq ft

COST
USD 316,000

ENERGY CONSUMPTION
0.9 kWh/sq ft/year

PROGRAM
Single-family residence

Photography © Peter Aaron/ESTO

The architect and artist Adam Kalkin was inspired by
upcycling for the design of this home. This concept
was inspired by the book *Cradle to Cradle: Remaking
the Way We Make Things* by M. Braungart and W.
McDonough, a manifesto on ecodesign.

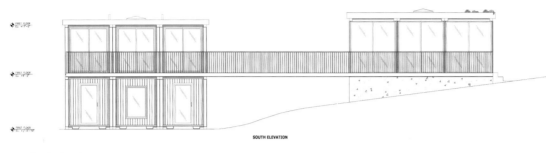

South elevation

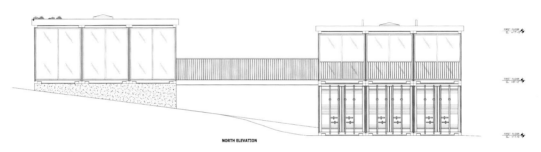

North elevation

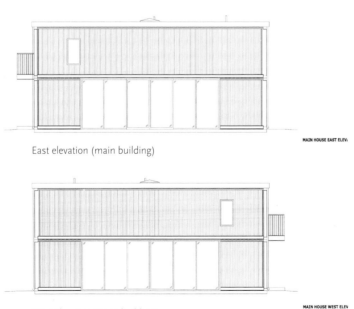

East elevation (main building)

West elevation (main building)

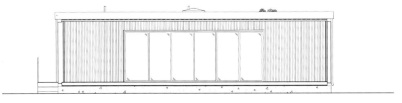

East elevation (extension)

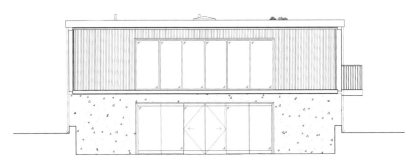

West elevation (extension)

An enthusiast of reusing shipping containers for architectural purposes throughout his career, Kalkin combined his knowledge of logic and mathematics, with his environmental awareness and sustainability principles to convert these industrial elements into a pleasant home.

Upper level (main building)

Upper level (extension)

Lower level (main building)

Lower level (extension)

TALIESIN MOD.FAB

Scottsdale, AZ, USA   2009

Nearly one hundred years ago, Frank Lloyd Wright launched a pioneer system of building prefabricated homes using precutting techniques, with factory-made closets and other pieces, based on building techniques he had seen in Japan. Wright christened them American System-Built Houses. But the outbreak of World War I prevented him from designing and building more than a handful of these homes.

Drawing inspiration from this, Taliesin Mod.Fab is the result of a design-construction workshop given at the Frank Lloyd Wright School of Architecture by Jennifer Siegal, a specialist in prefabricated construction. It is located on the school's desert campus, and students from the school participated in its construction.

This prototype is an example of a simple, elegant, and sustainable house for arid regions. Buildings formed in its style are initially made up of one bedroom, a bathroom, a kitchen, a living area and covered outdoor areas, although its open plan permits new spatial layouts.

The prototype is self-sufficient in its use of energy. It uses structural insulated panels (SIPs) and was designed to be connected to utilities or "unplugged." In the latter case, energy and water resources are provided by orientation, cross-ventilation, photovoltaic panels, rainwater collection, and gray water recycling.

The structure is designed to be transported by roadway. Prefabricated construction represents cost savings and a shorter building time.

ARCHITECT
Jennifer Siegal/Office of Mobile Design, Michael P. Johnson/Michael P. Johnson Design Studio

CLIENT
Frank Lloyd Wright School of Architecture, Taliesin West

COLLABORATORS
Graduate and undergraduate students of the Frank Lloyd Wright School of Architecture: Dakotah Apostolou, Ebbie Azimi, Thai Blackburn, Christian Butler, Jillian Brooks, Emil Crystal, Simon DeAguerro, Michael DesBarres, Daniel Dillow, Dave Frazee, Jeff Graham, Ryan Hewson, Erik Krautbauer, Todd Lehmenkuler, Russell Mahoney, Nick Mancusi, Marietta Pagkalou, Rebecca Peebles (project management), Lauren Rybinski, Taryn Seymour, Andrea Tejada, Maya Ward-Karet, Hui Ee Wong

TOTAL SURFACE AREA
600 sq ft

COST
USD 70,000

PROGRAM
Energy self-sufficient single-family residence

Photography © Bill Timmerman

The panels were set up on site to take advantage of solar energy during construction.

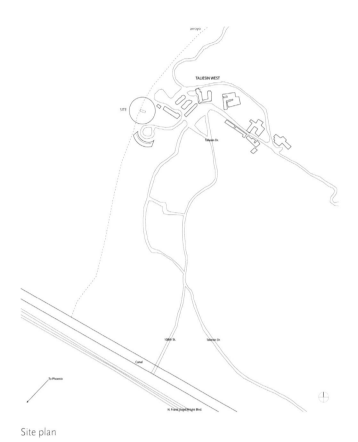

Site plan

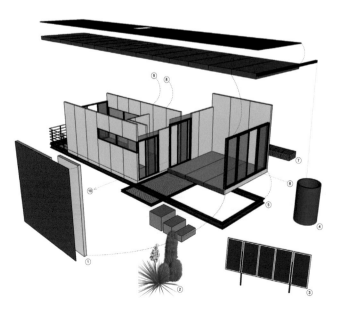

Exploded isometric view

1. SIPs on floor, walls, and roof
2. Cactus
3. Photovoltaic panels
4. Rainwater collection
5. 12 ft width adapted to transport
6. Passive heating-cooling
7. Fragment of gabion wall used as a bench
8. Water heater
9. Off-grid operation
10. South facing

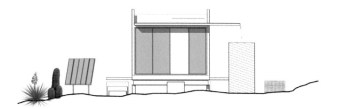

East elevation

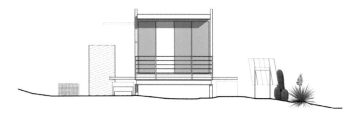

West elevation

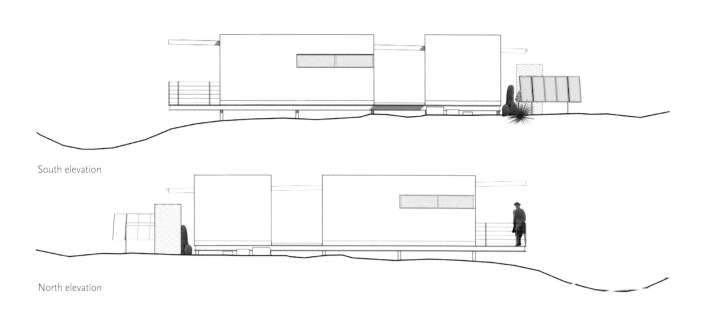

South elevation

North elevation

This prototype is currently being used as a guest
house, with furnishings donated by the Design Within
Reach studio.

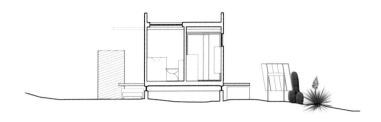

West section

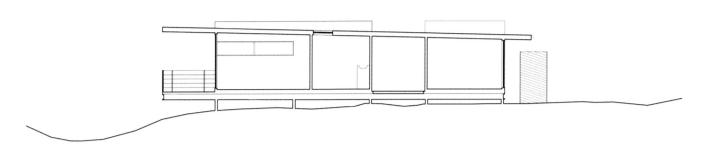

North section

Plan

PALMS HOUSE

Venice, CA, USA   2008

This residence is on a narrow property in a residential area of Venice, California. It features covered terraces and a small courtyard, which provides its owners with privacy.

The floor plan, made up of fourteen modules, is rectangular and laid out over two levels. The design consists of three bedrooms, two full bathrooms, a toilet room, a living-dining area, a double-height kitchen, an outdoor eating area, and a terrace. Large glazed expanses on the south-facing facade let natural light in and provide a visual connection between the building's interior and exterior.

The dwelling incorporates a number of environmental features, such as a recyclable steel frame and structural insulated panels (SIPs) that reduce heating needs by 12%–14%. It uses triple-pane insulated glazing, natural materials, low-VOC paints, and cross-ventilation systems.

The building's prefabricated construction system considerably reduced its environmental impact during building. The main prefabricated elements of the house are the recycled steel structural modules, metal panel cladding, wood flooring, walnut cabinetry, CaesarStone countertops, denim insulation, and the formaldehyde-free MDF in its furnishings.

Prefabrication also made the construction process faster. It took five months to build—three months in the factory, two months to assemble—and six weeks for finishes and landscaping.

ARCHITECT
Marmol Radziner Prefab

CLIENT
Leo Marmol and Alisa Becket

TOTAL SURFACE AREA
2,800 sq ft (interior), 700 sq ft (exterior)

PROGRAM
Single-family residence with outdoor space, 3 bedrooms, 2 full bathrooms, and a carport

Photography © David Lena

The house has exterior wood cladding. The use of laminated panels on the main facade protects the interior from being exposed to the street, but as it allows light to pass, it keeps the open feel proposed in the design.

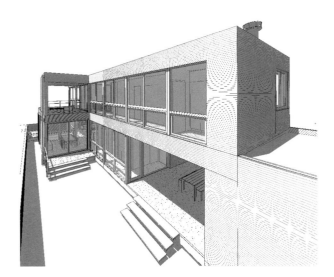

Rendering

Computer illustrations

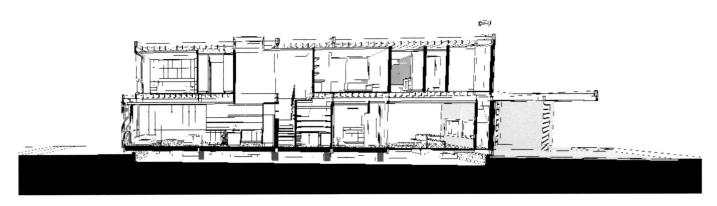

Section

The furnishings in the living area and kitchen are
handmade in walnut. The floors are concrete on the
lower floor and feature American walnut on the upper
level. The beds are incorporated into the bedroom
furnishings.

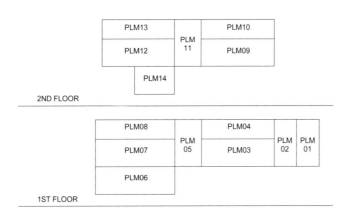

Module layout by floor

Lower level / upper level

SOLAR ACTIVE HOUSE

Kraig-Überfeld, Austria 2009

This prototype home, designed for an Austrian solar technology manufacturer, complies with requirements similar to those of the PassivHaus standard, such as good facade insulation and a bioclimatic design that favors solar heat gain.

The home is self-sufficient in energy. It produces all of the energy it consumes to achieve a zero net-energy balance. The south frontage gains solar energy by means of vertical openings and the picture window found on the lower level. Another active strategy is formed by the solar thermal panels integrated into the roof, and the photovoltaic panels used for electricity generation. In warm weather, the south-facing openings are protected from overheating by a fixed brise-soleil that forms 400 sq ft of photovoltaic panels. In winter, a heat pump provides comfort on extremely cold days. Otherwise, radiant heating is designed under skirting boards and flooring to heat areas of the house. The high degree of insulation achieved with triple glazing and heat-recovery ventilation reduces heat loss drastically.

The energy for heating, hot water, ventilation, and to power home appliances and the heat pump are compensated with power from the photovoltaic panels and the heat-recovery systems so that consumption is zero. The building is equipped with windows that open automatically only when oxygen levels are too low or when there is too much moisture in the air.

ARCHITECT
Architekturbüro Reinberg

CLIENT
Sonnenkraft Österreich Vertriebs GmbH

TOTAL SURFACE AREA
1,614 sq ft

COST
Showroom house; no market price

PROGRAM
Prototype single-family residence

Photography © Sonnenkraft Österreich, Horst Danner

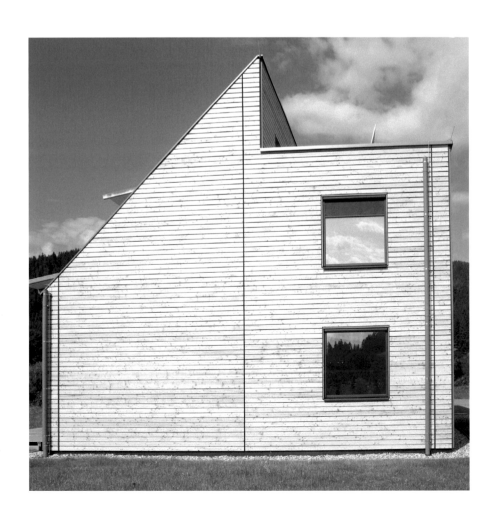

The building features a larch wood and glass skin
and a roof made from a material called Eternit.
The interiors walls are rendered in marl, a detritus
sedimentary material with equal parts of sand, silt,
and clay particles.

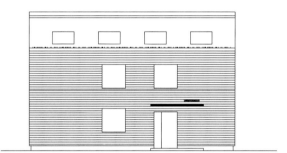

North elevation

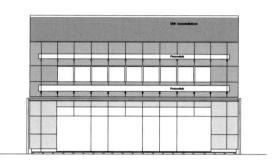

South elevation

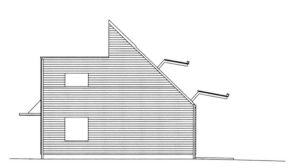

West elevation

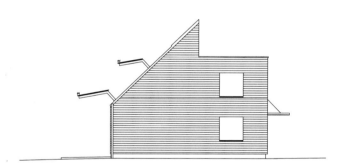

East elevation

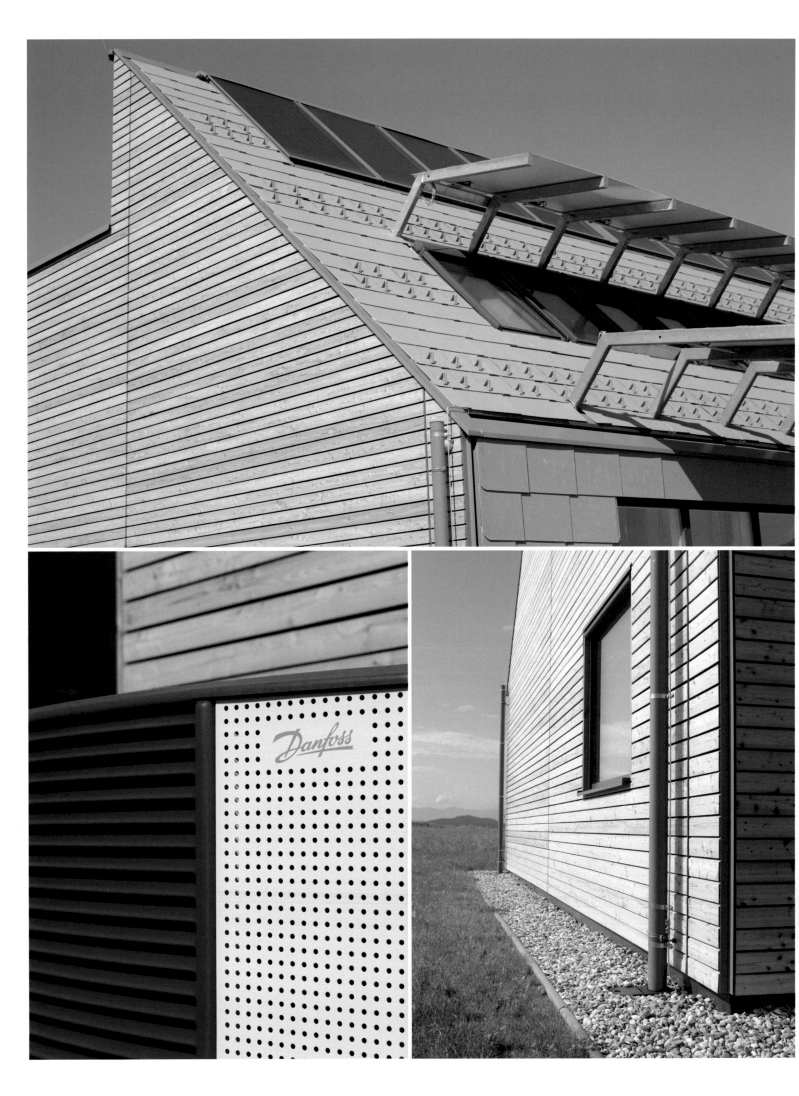

The house features 264 sq ft of thermal solar panels, with storage for household hot water (in the plant room and on the lower level) and a heat pump run on solar power.

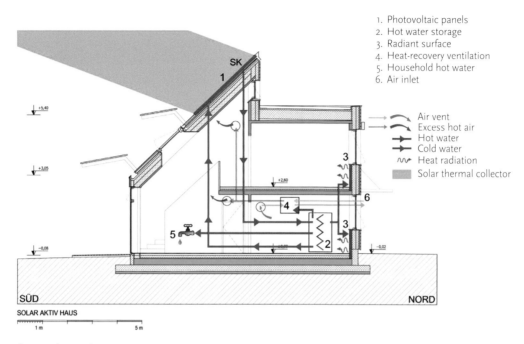

1. Photovoltaic panels
2. Hot water storage
3. Radiant surface
4. Heat-recovery ventilation
5. Household hot water
6. Air inlet

→⌐ Air vent
→⌐ Excess hot air
➡ Hot water
➡ Cold water
〜 Heat radiation
▨ Solar thermal collector

SÜD   NORD

SOLAR AKTIV HAUS
1 m   5 m

Section showing heating system

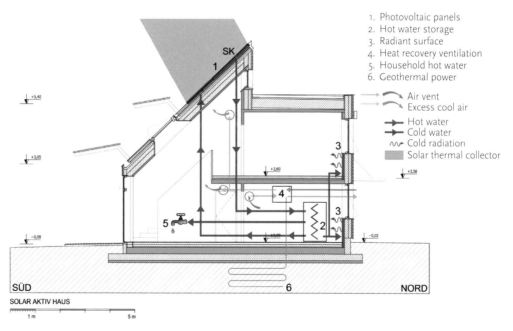

1. Photovoltaic panels
2. Hot water storage
3. Radiant surface
4. Heat recovery ventilation
5. Household hot water
6. Geothermal power

→⌐ Air vent
→⌐ Excess cool air
➡ Hot water
➡ Cold water
〜 Cold radiation
▨ Solar thermal collector

SÜD   NORD

SOLAR AKTIV HAUS
1 m   5 m

Section showing cooling system

NOMADHOME TREND PRIVATE 77c

Seekirchen am Wallersee, Austria   2005

Nomadhome is a patented flexible building system using 118 sq ft modules. The system, invented by Gerold Peham, is a design for a totally flexible house as a symbol of the twenty-first century. The modules are for sale, but since they are easily constructed and deconstructed, they can be installed on rented land.

Nomadhome structures can be used for commercial or residential purposes. The modules are interchangeable and extendable. A structure can be disassembled in two to three days and the modules can be transported by road.

The use of sandwich panels for the frame and systems installations that can be adapted from one module to another enable an unlimited number of modules to be added to extend the original.

The basic Nomadhome structure is roughly 540 sq ft, although it appears larger owing to Peham's skill in laying out interior spaces without partition walls, as in an industrial loft. Its outer cladding can be any one of a number of materials: aluminum, copper, corrugated steel, larch, or PVC panels colored to order. Interior color schemes also vary according to demand.

The electrical, home automation, and air-conditioning systems are modular and extendable as a result of the connection used. There is also a possibility that in the future, the modules will come equipped with solar-energy and rainwater-capturing systems.

ARCHITECT
Hobby A., Schuster & Maul, Gerold Peham

CLIENT
Gerold Peham

COLLABORATORS
Fill Metallbau GmbH, Aktivbau

TOTAL SURFACE AREA
947 sq ft

COST
USD 257,500

ENERGY CONSUMPTION
87 kWh/sq ft/year

CERTIFICATION
C rating (European building energy certification)

PROGRAM
Single-family housing

Photography © Marc Haader

Gerold Peham's practice imagined a future with
communities or towns made up of a succession of
Nomadhomes.

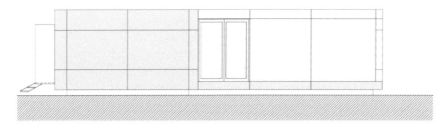

Southwest elevation

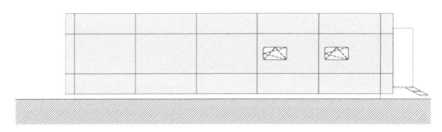

Southeast elevation

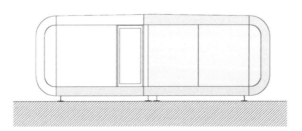

Northeast elevation

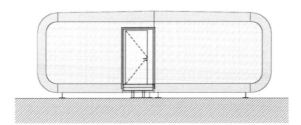

Northwest elevation

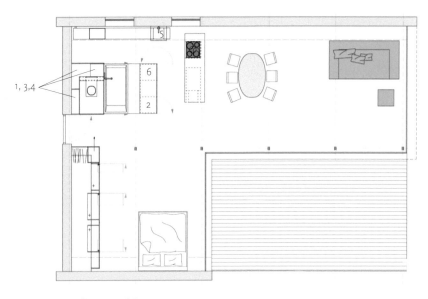

1. Machine room
2. Washing machine
3. Air-conditioning system
4. Electrical system
5. Sink
6. Refrigerator

Plan of basic module

ADRIANCE HOUSE / 12 CONTAINER HOUSE

Blue Hill, ME, USA   2002

Like for the Quik House, Adam Kalkin was inspired by the concept of upcycling for the design of this vacation home for a couple with two children.

There had already been experiences with the use of containers as public housing in cities such as London and Amsterdam. The house is laid out on a rectangular floor plan with two wings. Six containers were used on the lower level and six more upstairs. The east and west facades are fully glazed. The main artery of the house is formed by a lobby-type space with a concrete floor. From there, two staircases, one north and the other south, lead to private areas on the upper level.

The container structure is roofed with galvanized steel and features two skylights above each stairwell, letting in natural light.

The final solution formally revives the aesthetics of a hangar, and features the economical, sustainable, and social characteristics of the architecture with containers.

ARCHITECT
Adam Kalkin/Quik Build

CLIENT
Anne and Matt Adriance

COLLABORATORS
Butler Corporation

TOTAL SURFACE AREA
4,000 sq ft

COST
USD 490,000

ENERGY CONSUMPTION
1.5 kWh/sq ft/year

PROGRAM
Vacation home for a family of four

Photography © Peter Aaron/ESTO

Construction with containers has a strong environmental focus, as it extends the useful life of a waste product from the transport sector, while reducing the amount of waste created in construction owing to its rapid assembly process.

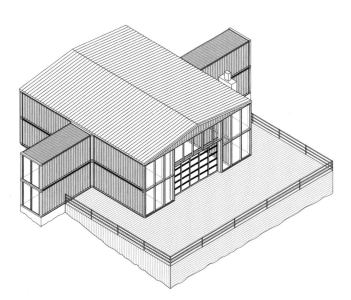

Southeast isometric view

West elevation

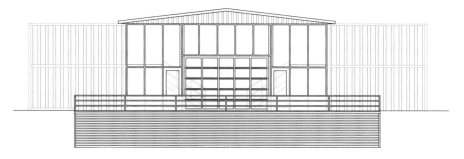

East elevation

1

485

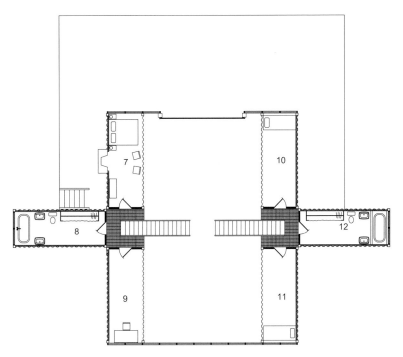

Upper level

1. Library
2. Kitchen
3. Playroom
4. Bathroom
5. Office
6. Guest bedroom
7. Master bedroom
8. Master bathroom
9. Office
10–11. Children's bedroom
12. Children's bathroom

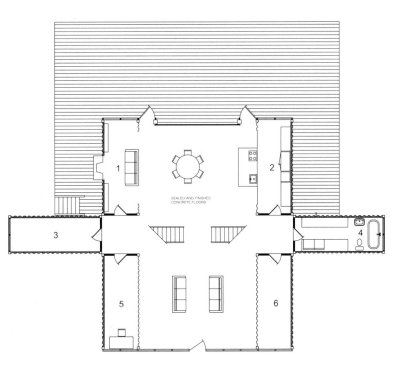

Lower level

REDONDO BEACH HOUSE

Redondo Beach, CA, USA   2007

This house, located in a suburb of Los Angeles, is made from eight 40 ft ISO shipping containers, which provide the residence with a flexible distribution. The availability of this type of disused shipping containers in the United States combined with the presence of aerospace technology has led to the creation of a variety of hybrid houses that rely on a combination of the two.

The architects' industrial-style modular building system for the containers maximizes effective construction. In this case, the containers were brought to the site with preinstalled mechanical, electrical, and sanitation systems. The building's thermal insulation is a ceramic material sprayed on its inside and outside surfaces, similar to that used by NASA for its space shuttles. The roof consists of prefabricated metal panels, while the sides are made from acrylic sheets. The bioclimatic design enhances cross-ventilation and greatly reduces the need for air-conditioning. The energy consumed during construction was 400 kW per container.

Using shipping containers saves time (the project required only 180 construction days) and avoids the waste produced using conventional building practices. They are stronger than conventional wood or steel frames and can withstand meteorological events and earthquakes, both common in this location. Their steel structures are mold proof, fireproof, and termite proof, and their use reduces the need to exploit the Earth's iron reserves.

ARCHITECT
DeMaria Design Associates

TOTAL SURFACE AREA
3,200 sq ft (living space), 550 sq ft (garage)

COST
Prefabrication, transportation, and assembly: USD 418,000

PROGRAM
Residence made from eight shipping containers

Photography © Andre Movsesyan, Christian Kienapfel

The living area has a 20 ft height and features folding
hangar doors. These doors also serve as a canopy
when they are folded up.

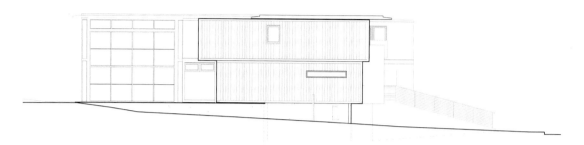

North Elevation

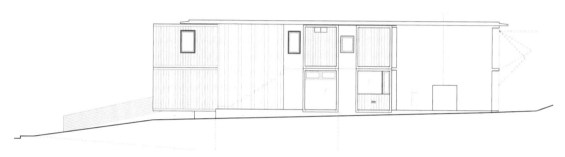

South Elevation

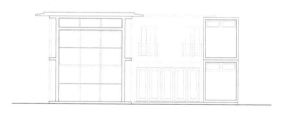

East Elevation

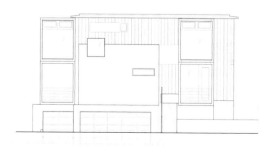

West Elevation

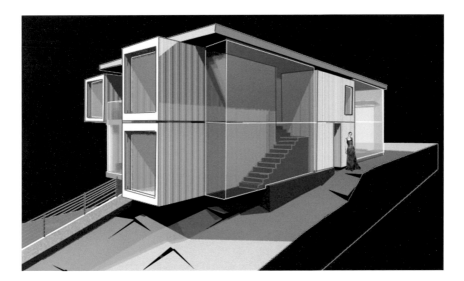

Rendering

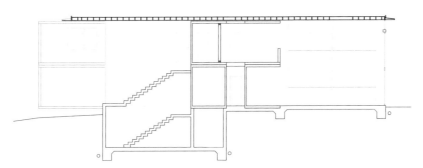

South section

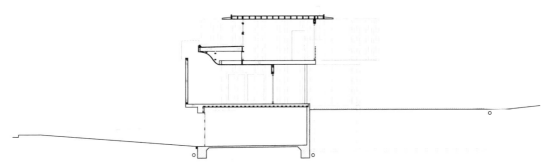

Cross-section

70% of the building work was carried out in a factory.
DeMaria describes this style of home as a "new
residential product line." The price of the home is
USD 355 per sq ft.

Second floor

1. Guest room
2. Laundry
3. Balcony
4. Bathroom
5. Bedroom
6. Reception
7. Wardrobe
8. Master bedroom
9. Wardrobe
10. Main bathroom

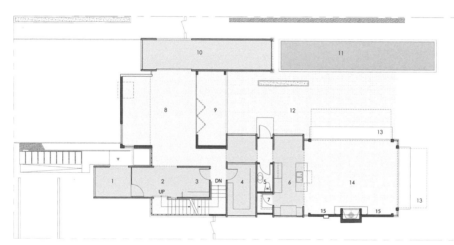

First floor

1. Porch
2. Reception
3. Storeroom
4. Entrance
5. Toilet
6. Kitchen
7. Pantry
8. Study
9. Porch
10. Open-air entertainment area
11. Swimming pool
12. Patio
13. Hangar doors
14. Living area
15. Climbing wall

Basement

1. Garage
2. Wardrobe
3. Games room

LANDSCAPE

BALLAST POINT PARK

Sydney, NSW, Australia   2008

This park is located in an industrial area on the Birchgrove Peninsula in the harbor suburb of Balmain. Between 1920 and 2002, the Caltex oil company used the site to store fuel for ships, meaning that the area was potentially contaminated by fuel. The site had also been previously used as a quarry for ship ballasts, hence the name.

According to the landscape architects, there were three motivations behind the park's design: 1) to create a large recreational space; 2) to provide good signposting for visitors' ease of use; and 3) to reflect the history of the site in the park (and in fact, traces of the area's history can be found during a walk around the park).

Only the bare frame remains of the storage tank, which has been renovated.

New elements, such as wind turbines and graphics, have been added to the park. From a distance, noticeable features of the park are the green color of its lawn, the rock quarry (in use at the turn of the twentieth century), and remnants of the area's industrial past.

The design minimizes the ecological footprint of human settlement without disregarding its effects. The new features of the park enable storm water biofiltration to occur and feature recycled materials. They are self-sufficient in energy production and usage, which is generated by the wind turbines on the site.

The wind turbines produce a yearly total of 1,752 kWh/year, which is used as energy. This calculation is based on an average wind speed of 10 ft/s.

ARCHITECT
McGregor Coxall

CLIENT
Sydney Harbour Foreshore Authority

COLLABORATORS
Deuce Design (interpretative elements and wayfinding signage)

TOTAL SURFACE AREA
270,000 sq ft

COST
USD 7,495,720

ENERGY CONSUMPTION
0.024 kWh/sq ft/year (night lighting only)

PROGRAM
Public park on former port and industrial site

Photography © Agnese Sanvito, Christian Brochert

The retaining walls are made from the rubble found on the site and are kept in place with wire netting, representing a positive environmental aspect, as this has done away with the need to extract and transport building materials from other parts of Sydney.

Ground plan

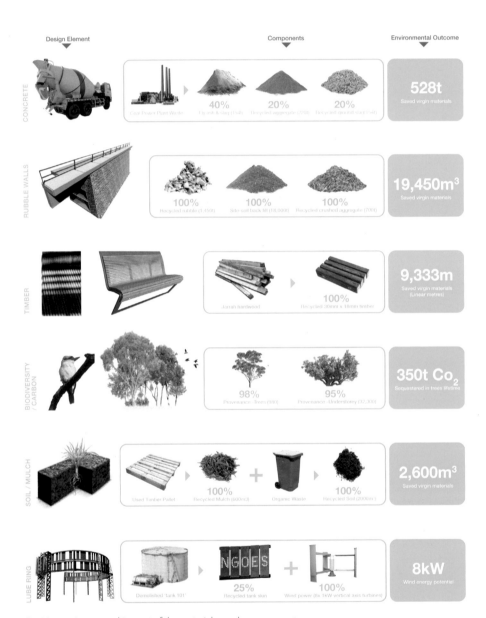

Positive environmental impact of the materials used

This unusual system of wind turbines makes the park self-sufficient in energy. The turbines' sculptural nature makes them landmarks, and they can be used for educational purposes.

THE HIGH LINE

New York, NY, USA
2009 (section I)–2010 (section II under construction)

The High Line was built in the 1930s as part of the West Side Improvement project, a large-scale public and private infrastructure plan for this New York City district. But its stretch of railroad, which passed through central Manhattan, was the cause of numerous deaths between 1851 and 1929 (and actually came to be known as Death Avenue). So in order to eliminate the accidents caused by the street-level crossings, the track was raised 30 ft above the ground for thirteen miles by the New York Central Railroad. Nonetheless, it became disused in 1980.

The initiative to turn the line into a public park was led by the Friends of the High Line, an association formed in 1999 when this historical structure was threatened with demolition. The project gained definitive backing from city authorities in 2002. CSX Transportation, Inc. donated the section south of Thirtieth Street to the city in 2005. As a result, there is now an urban public space that colors Manhattan's skyline green, but without silencing the rumble of traffic below.

The park has restrictions on the hours it is open to the public. Drinking alcohol is not permitted, nor are bicycles, skateboards, or dogs. It combines landscape elements with architectural ones, such as stairs and elevators every two or three blocks.

The first section of the High Line park was opened in 2009. Once the pending sections are complete, the park will have a length of approximately 1.5 miles.

ARCHITECT
James Corner Field Operations, Diller Scofidio + Renfro

CLIENT
City of New York and Friends of the High Line

COLLABORATORS
Buro Happold (structural and MEP engineering), Robert Silman Associates (structural engineering and historic preservation), Piet Oudolf (planting design), L'Observatoire International (lighting), Pentagram Design, Inc. (signage), Northern Design (irrigation), GRB Services, Inc. (environmental engineering and site remediation), Philip Habib & Associates (civil and traffic engineering), Pine & Swallow Associates, Inc. (soil science), ETM Associates (public space management)

TOTAL SURFACE AREA
753,500 sq ft

COST
USD 151,000,000 (Sections I and II)

PROGRAM
Public park created from former rail trestle

Drawings Design by James Corner Field Operations and Diller Scofidio + Renfro, courtesy of the City of New York

Photography © Iwan Baan, Joel Sternfeld

In existence since 1929, the High Line operated as an elevated railroad between 1934 and 1980. Between 1980 and 2002 it was threatened with demolition, a situation that was averted with the park project, which saw the first section open in 2009.

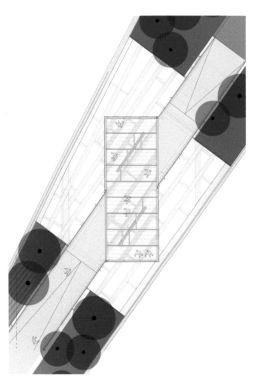

Plan of one section

Section

Section of elevated walkway

512

The pedestrian space still has sections of rail tracks to preserve the memory of its historical past. The plantings on the structure include grass, shrubs, and small trees. The space features benches and movable wooden seating for visitors to rest.

Rendering

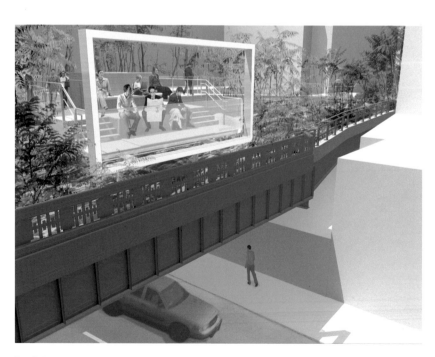

Rendering

ECOBOULEVARD IN VALLECAS

Madrid, Spain   2006

This project consists of the design for a pedestrian walkway in a new residential suburb being built in the outskirts of Madrid. Its intention is to implement bioclimatic strategies on the main avenue of the UE1 sector of a new Vallecas town development. Its innovative urban design experience aims to enhance the feeling of atmospheric comfort, to promote social interaction, and to be more sustainable than conventional urban growth models.

Environmental criteria were established for all parts of the project: the materials used (mostly recycled), the use of renewable energies, passive air-conditioning systems, resource optimization, enhancement of social function, and a new asymmetrical vehicular traffic roadway layout.

Ecosistema Urbano designed three "air trees" that operate as supports for a number of different user activities. They are designed to act like groves of the future; after a certain time, they should be taken down, leaving spaces like clearings in a forest.

The air tree is a light, dismountable, and self-sufficient structure. It only consumes the energy it is able to produce by means of a photovoltaic solar-energy capture system. This technology borrows from greenhouse heating and cooling techniques to achieve more comfortable temperatures for its area of the street (8 °C–10 °C/46 °F–50 °F cooler than the rest of the street in summer).

ARCHITECT
Ecosistema Urbano

CLIENT
Madrid City Council Housing and Land Authority and the European Union (LIFE-2002 program)

TOTAL SURFACE AREA
296,000 sq ft

COST
USD 3,522,000

ENERGY CONSUMPTION
0.0022 kWh/sq ft/year (12 kWh per tree)

PROGRAM
Pedestrian walkway

Photography © Emilio P. Doiztua, Roland Halbe

The structure is extremely light and totally
dismountable. It is also self-sufficient in that it only
consumes the energy produced by its photovoltaic
panels.

Color sketch

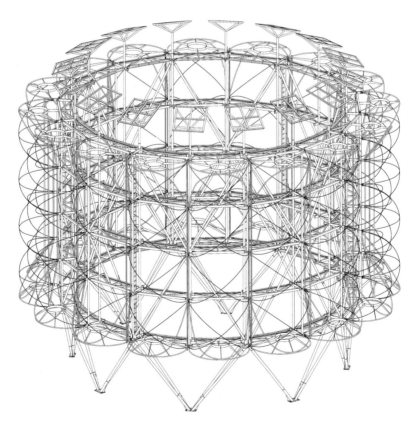

Isometric view

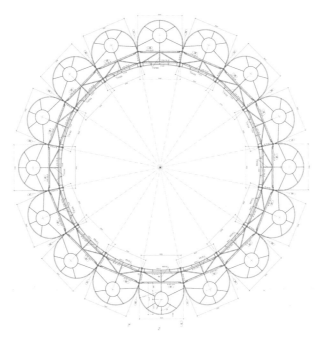

Overhead view of the structure

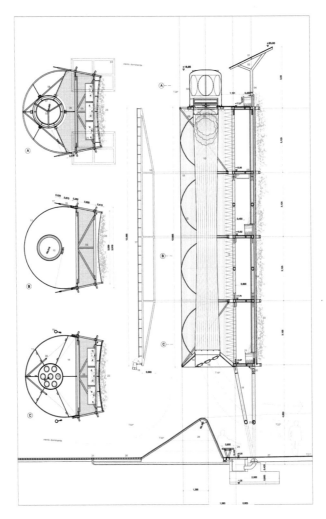

Construction details

Seen from inside, a mesh structure acts as a filter
and creates a shady space—a type of "plant theater,"
which gives visitors a completely different view of their
urban surroundings by means of a bioclimatic screen.

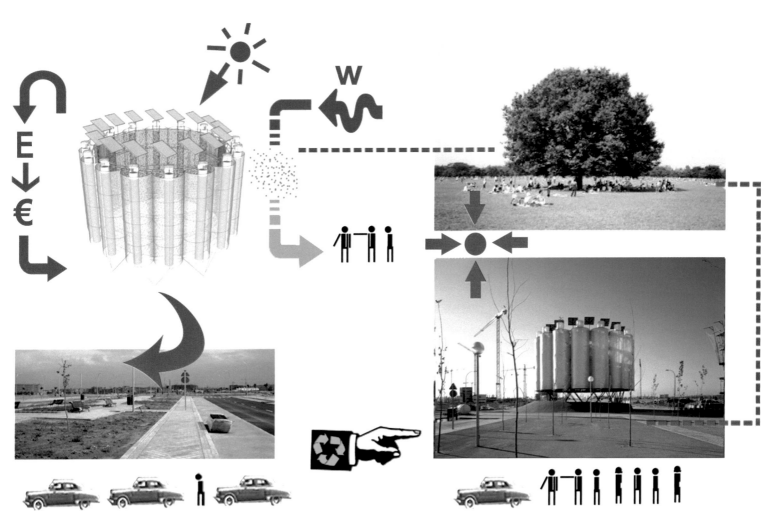

Energy and water circulation cycle chart

ALEXANDRA ARCH & FOREST WALK

Singapore, Singapore   2008

This project consists of three parts: Alexandra Arch, Forest Walk, and a walking trail.

The local planning authorities wanted this project to connect hills in the Southern Ridges area of Singapore, comprising Mount Faber, Telok Blangah Hill, and Kent Ridge, to create an uninterrupted corridor in the midst of urban districts to provide the public with access to nature.

The Alexandra Arch rises 20 ft above Alexandra Road. It is supported by concrete piers, and the deck is surfaced in granite.

The elevated forest walkway stands between 10 ft and 60 ft above ground level. It consists of galvanized steel pillars, structure, and mesh. Its one mile length winds upward for 190 ft from the urban area where the arched bridge is located over a valley, along a cliff, across a plateau, through forested and terraced areas, passing from one landscape to another, following the chain of hills until it reaches the highest point in the park. Parallel to the walkway, a trail along the ground takes a similar path. It is one mile in length and 7 ft wide, with a change in altitude of 224 ft over its course. The trail is gravel lined with granite stones.

Despite its location in an urban area, this project brings people in contact with nature, while providing a corridor through an area of hilly terrain.

ARCHITECT
Look Architects

CLIENT
Urban Redevelopment Authority of Singapore

COLLABORATORS
Ecas-EJ Consultants, Buro Happold (civil and structural engineering), HY M&E Consultancy Services (mechanical and electrical engineering), JIA Quantity Surveyors & Project Managers (quantity surveyor)

TOTAL SURFACE AREA
3,450 sq ft (Alexandra Arch), 34,500 sq ft (Forest Walk), 3,450 sq ft (trail)

COST
USD 9,000,000

PROGRAM
Pedestrian walkway, footbridge, and trail

Photography © Amir Sultan, Tim Nolan

The zigzagging steel structure blends with the leafy
forest surroundings.

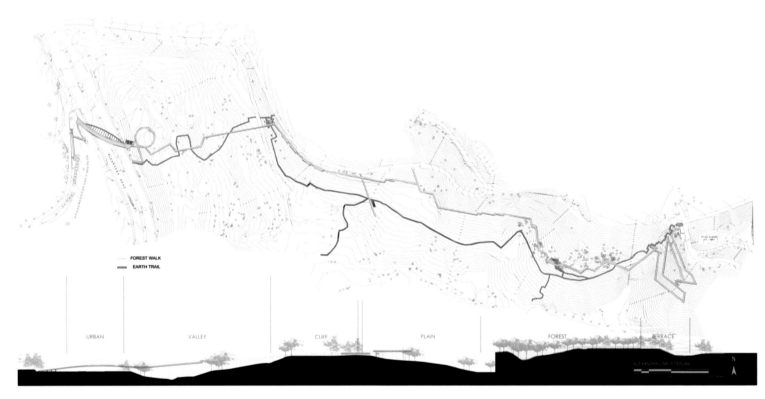

FOREST WALK
EARTH TRAIL

URBAN   VALLEY   CLIFF   PLAIN   FOREST   TERRACE

Ground plan

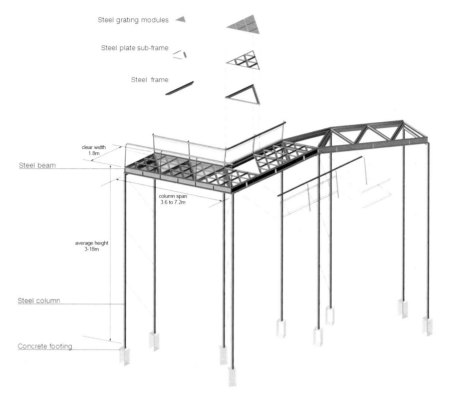

Steel grating modules

Steel plate sub-frame

Steel frame

clear width
1.8m

Steel beam

column span
3.6 to 7.2m

average height
3-18m

Steel column

Concrete footing

Diagram of walkway

The arch is at one end of the walkway across from Telok Blangah Hill and spans Alexandra Road, a thoroughfare leading to downtown Singapore, at a height of 20 ft.

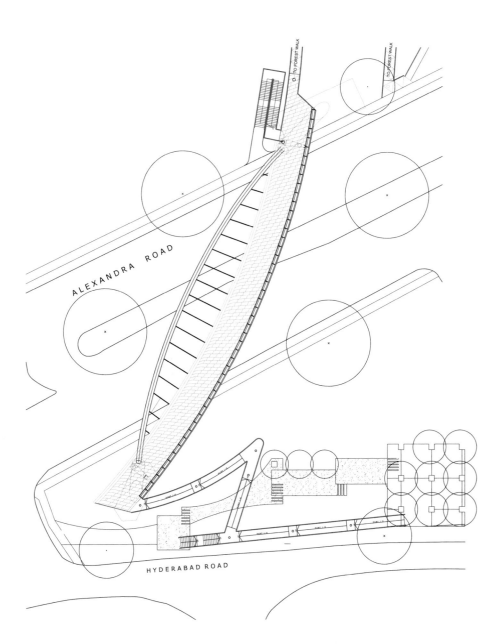

Alexandra Arch ground plan

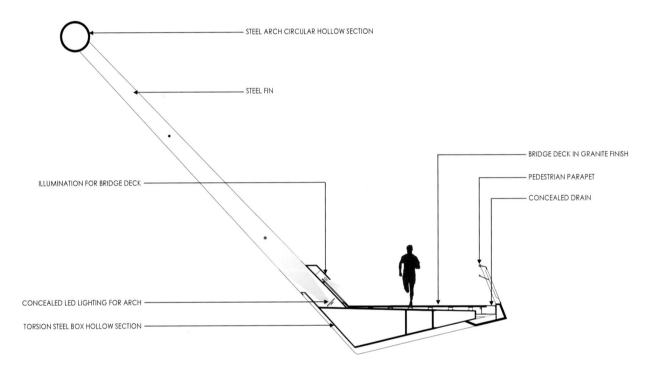

STEEL ARCH CIRCULAR HOLLOW SECTION

STEEL FIN

BRIDGE DECK IN GRANITE FINISH

PEDESTRIAN PARAPET

CONCEALED DRAIN

ILLUMINATION FOR BRIDGE DECK

CONCEALED LED LIGHTING FOR ARCH

TORSION STEEL BOX HOLLOW SECTION

Alexandra Arch section

QUEENS BOTANICAL GARDEN

New York, NY, USA   2007

Located a few miles east of Manhattan, this project is the redesign of a public park that was built for the 1939 World's Fair. Key changes included the creation of a new visitor and administration center, a water feature design, a horticulture and maintenance building, and a relocation of the parking lot.

The new design makes full use of the site's collected rainwater, reducing surface runoff to a minimum by means of different strategies such as channeling the rainwater falling on the 16,000 sq ft roof of the new administration building and capturing runoff water for water features and watering. Sumps placed around the 46,000 sq ft parking area

hold rainwater. Gray water produced in the building is collected, treated, and re-used for watering.

The water features serve as a directional guide for visitors arriving at the main entrance of the park, and connect the new visitor and administration center visually with the surrounding vegetation.

Queens Botanical Garden is a meeting place for global preservation, local sustainability, and the importance of cultural practices related to the preservation of natural resources. In a world where water may be scarce owing to improper use and widespread agricultural practices that pollute, this public space is also a place for reflection.

ARCHITECT
Atelier Dreiseitl

CLIENT
Queens Botanical Garden and City of New York

COLLABORATORS
Conservation Design Forum (Chicago), BKSK (New York)

TOTAL SURFACE AREA
39 acres

COST
USD 13,000,000 (building and public space)

CERTIFICATION
USGBC LEED platinum

PROGRAM
Integration of public and recreation spaces in areas of mixed use

Photography © Atelier Dreiseitl, ESTO

The visitor center terrace is an outdoor meeting place, made picture-perfect by its roof canopy and views of the gardens. The building is located on the site where the old parking lot stood, which is bordered by oaks and conifers of considerable age.

1. Green roof
2. Watercourse
3. Entrance plaza
4. Fountain
5. Surface runoff
6. Water channel
7. Pool
8. Roof canopy
9. Visitor and administration center roof
10. Cleansing biotope
11. Natural sump
12. Drain
13. To the sanitation system
14. Plant room
15. Rainwater tank (24,000 gallons)

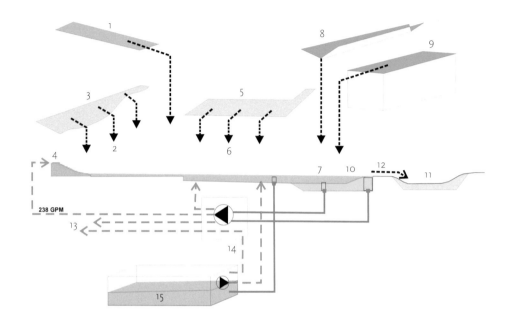

Rainwater collection chart

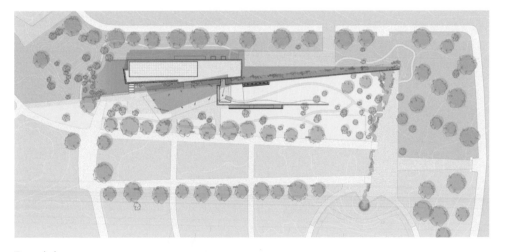

Ground plan

Retention area in 1–10 years
Retention area in 1–100 years

Rainwater retention

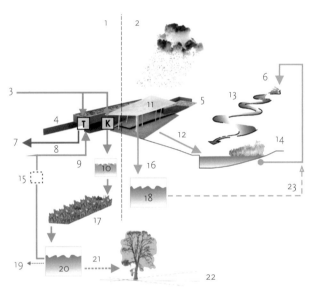

Water cycle chart

1. Gray water system
2. Rainwater system
3. Potable water
4. Nonpotable water
5. Green roof
6. Recirculated rainwater
7. Drain
8. Nonpotable water for use in toilets
9. Tank installation
10. Gray water
11. Water-collecting roof canopy
12. Surface runoff
13. Water feature
14. Cleansing biotope
15. Additional disinfection
16. Collected rainwater
17. Artificial wetlands
18. Rainwater storage tank
19. Emergency drainage to city sanitation network
20. Storage tank
21. Excess water
22. Ground watering
23. Excess water
T. Toilets
K. Kitchen

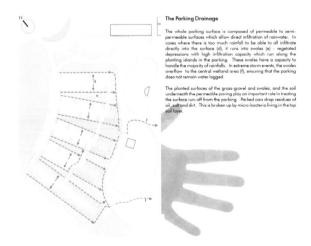

The Parking Drainage

The whole parking surface is composed of permeable to semi-permeable surfaces which allow direct infiltration of rainwater. In cases where there is too much rainfall to be able to all infiltrate directly into the surface (d), it runs into swales (e) - vegetated depressions with high infiltration capacity which run along the planting islands in the parking. These swales have a capacity to handle the majority of rainfalls. In extreme storm events, the swales overflow to the central wetland area (f), ensuring that the parking does not remain water logged.

The planted surfaces of the grass-gravel and swales, and the soil underneath the permeable paving play an important role in treating the surface run-off from the parking. Parked cars drop residues of oil, salt and dirt. This is broken up by micro-bacteria living in the top soil layer.

Parking lot drainage system plan

Color rendering of aerial view of parking lot

LONG ISLAND (GREEN) CITY /
SILVERCUP STUDIOS GREEN ROOF

Long Island City, NY, USA   2002 – 2005

Balmori Associates received a commission from a Long Island real estate developer to carry out a feasibility study for greening the roofs of certain factories on Long Island. The aim was to create smart infrastructure that would provide economic and environmental benefits. The action was to be undertaken in the Queens District of Long Island City, an emerging cultural neighborhood, where a series of buildings required renovations on their roofs.

Balmori set up a pilot project using the roof at Silvercup Studios to monitor the possible development of the project on a greater scale. Aided by staff from Pennsylvania State University and a green roof consultant, the architects obtained data from roofs where there were both green and unplanted modules, be-tween the end of 2005 and 2006. The results showed the regulating effect of green layers with regard to the performance of the building in both summer and winter months.

The study concluded that a roof's absorption of heat from the sun in summer can be reduced 90%–100% by greening, with reduction in energy use for air-conditioning by 30%–50% in summer and in the vicinity of 50%–100% in spring and fall.

Other points in favor of planted green roofs are that they can manage rainwater, given that they lessen runoff, absorbing and storing more water, releasing it later, a little at a time. Additionally, the released water has lower heavy metal concentrations, from such things as zinc, than the runoff from a conventional roof.

ARCHITECT
Balmori Associates

CLIENT
Silvercup Studios

TOTAL SURFACE AREA
11,700,000 sq ft (Long Island Green City), 35,000 sq ft (Silvercup Studios Green Roof)

PROGRAM
Proposal for a network of green roofs

Photography © Mark Dye

The green roof at Silvercup Studios is only the first in a
series of green roofs planned for Long Island City this
decade.

Site plan

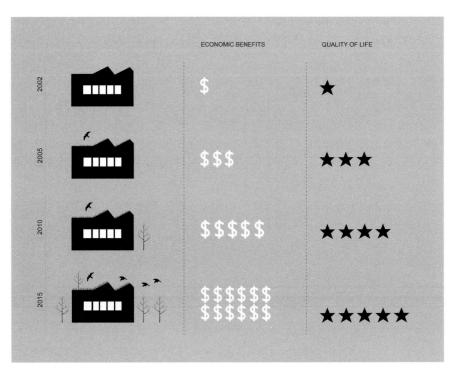

Forecast of economic and quality-of-life benefits

WHAT IF
LONG ISLAND CITY
WERE A
GREEN CITY?

SMART INFRASTRUCTURE

544

Vegetating a roof is an action of an urban nature that can be about improvements in health for citizens, which occurs by regulating the temperature in their homes, while benefitting both plant and animal wildlife.

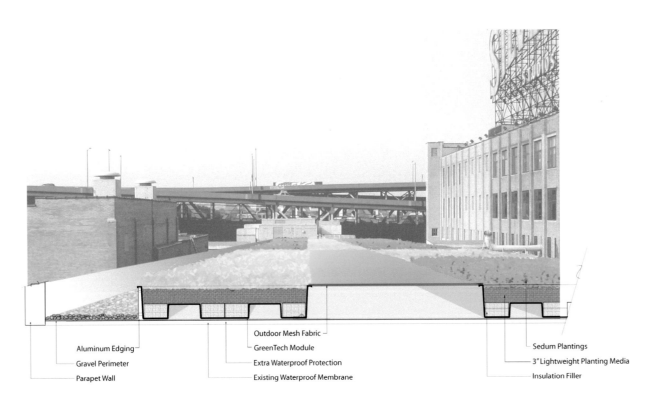

Green potential of Long Island City (NY)

Aluminum Edging
Gravel Perimeter
Parapet Wall

Outdoor Mesh Fabric
GreenTech Module
Extra Waterproof Protection
Existing Waterproof Membrane

Sedum Plantings
3" Lightweight Planting Media
Insulation Filler

A green roof reduces daily fluctuations in temperature and acts as a solar canopy, lengthening the life of the roof membrane. The maximum daily fluctuation in the roof membrane temperature was 41 °F at the green roof membrane.

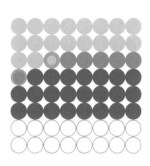

36% Built Area

Total Built Area 17,328,429 ft² (29%)
Unbuilt Area 12,353,073 (25%)
Queens West 3,224,272 (6.7%)

55% Greenspace Potential

Total Possible Green Area 26,678,743ft² (55%)
667 acres

Green potential of Long Island City (NY)

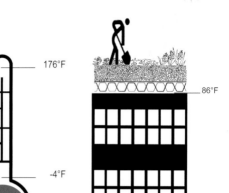

Benefits for the building

1. The temperatures on asphalt roofs can oscillate by 180 °F
2. Green roofs prevent extreme fluctuations

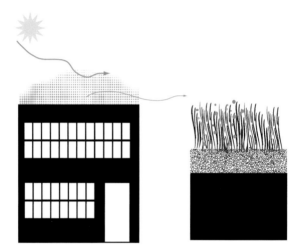

Benefits for air quality

1. The movement of warm air encourages the formation of suspended particles
2. Plants clean the air

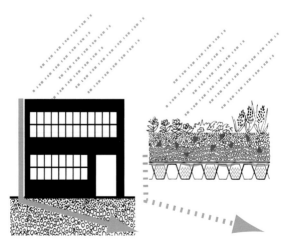

Benefits for rainwater

1 Reduces contaminated runoff
2. Absorbs and filters rainwater

HARNES LAGOONING PONDS

Harnes, France   2004

This project began as a 1992 study of a former coal mine in the vicinity of the Lens Canal in northern France by the European Coal and Steel Community (ECSC) to give new uses to large abandoned areas and to improve the quality of surface waters.

The development project consisted of two stages: 1) in 1996 the terrain was excavated to produce 4,300,000 cu ft of rubble, and various preparatory works were undertaken; 2) between 1994 and 2004, construction of the stabilization lagoon began, with emphasis placed on making it watertight, on hydraulics, and on the planting of vegetation.

Water treatment was a main focus, but the project was also given a number of other aims, including: reconstruction of wetlands; increasing local biodiversity; creation of a regional aquatic garden; new uses such as recreation area and new bathing area; and consolidation of the Lens Canal greenbelt.

The water is treated by means of lagooning, a system historically used in Arab countries. First, the water passes through a filter created by willows planted on a gravel bed, where the plants absorb part of the nitrogen (the willows here grow very quickly and need to be changed every three years). Then the water leaving this area, which still has phosphates and nitrates in it, is sent to filtering reed beds (other species such as *Typha angustifolia, Butomus umbellatus, Iris pseudacorus,* and *Epilobium hirsutum* are also used in the process). And finally, water reaches the large pond, covering 162,000 sq ft, which is safe for bathing, while also being a habitat for birds, frogs, insects, and bats.

ARCHITECT
AgencePaysages

CLIENT
Communauté d'Agglomération
Lens-Lievin

COLLABORATORS
F.U.L. (stabilization ponds), Burgeap (hydrogeology), and Berim (technical studies)

TOTAL SURFACE AREA
43 acres (13.6 acres of which are lagoons)

COST
USD 2,032,900

PROGRAM
Ecological restoration of a former mining area

Photography © AgencePaysages

The new urban park at Drocourt was possible owing to the recovery of 148 acres of coking works and 300 acres of slag heaps. The Harnes ponds are part of a 385-mile green corridor, including a Grand Randonnée hiking trail.

Operations on an image from 1950

1. Lagooning
2. Oxygenation and exposure to ultraviolet rays
3. Lagooning in basins containing aquatic plants
4. Courrières
5. Willow filtering
6. Water sent from the water treatment plant
7. Final lagooning stage
8. Future bathing area
9. Outflow into the Lens Canal

HARNES

1 Lagunage

2 Oxygénation
Exposition aux ultra-violets

3 Lagunage
dans les bassins plantés
de végétaux aquatiques

4 COURRIÈRES

9 Rejet dans le canal de Lens

5 Filtration dans
les taillis de saules

8 Future
zone de baignade

6 Rejet
de la station d'épuration

7 Lagunage de finition

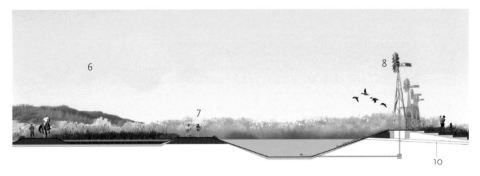

1. Filtering by willows planted on gravel
2. Input from the Fouquières water treatment plant
3. Short-cycle willow planting
4. Buildings
5. Aquatic plants
6. Lagooning in basins containing aquatic plants
7. Grass-covered dyke
8. Wind turbines
9. Oxygenation and exposure to ultraviolet rays
10. Channels
11. Cascade
12. Rocks
13. Topsoil
14. Schist ramp
15. Watertightness
16. Access to the Montigny Canal
17. Canal bridge
18. Different levels of drainage

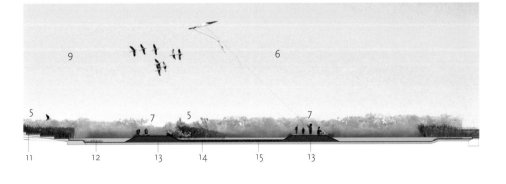

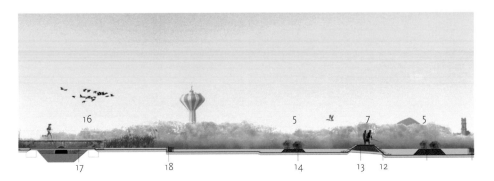

Sections of the lagooning and vegetation systems

URBANISM

TORONTO LOWER DON LANDS PARK

Toronto, Canada   Competition

Toronto's industrial past is represented by the factories and service areas at the mouth of the Don River, which at the time of their construction flowed into Lake Ontario through Ashbridge's Bay. Since then, the river's channel was altered owing to the construction of an industrial port and the building of roadway overpasses and rail infrastructure over the Don, which destroyed the existing ecosystem. The Lower Don Lands currently represent a void in the city, a disconnection between the river and what used to be its mouth.

The program for this design proposal was to create a new waterfront for Toronto combining recreational, cultural, and residential uses in a development where water and green spaces would bring about the appropriate conditions for life and civic enjoyment.

Weiss/Manfredi designed what they called "wandering ecologies." The regreening of this zone will involve the creation of new wetlands, which will serve as habitats for birds and aquatic wildlife, and facilities for water sports such as kayaking and fishing.

This project was designed in 2007 but did not materialize. One of the key features of the new park would have been the boardwalk and pier outlook that was to serve as a year-round venue for festivals and events, in addition to being a perfect vantage point to view the city's skyline.

ARCHITECT
Weiss/Manfredi

CLIENT
Toronto Waterfront Revitalization Corporation and City of Toronto

COLLABORATORS
Du Toit Allsopp Hillier (landscaping), Weidlinger Associates (structural engineering), McCormick Rankin Corporation (civil and structural engineering), Biohabitats (environmental restoration), Golder Associates, Ltd. (hydrogeological engineering)

TOTAL SURFACE AREA
100 acres

Renderings © Weiss/Manfredi

The plan for the new park was divided into six zones: the port lands, the boardwalk-pier outlook, the peninsula, a park, a plaza, and a wetlands zone. The park was designed so that traffic would be distributed by a network of paths, bicycle trails, and local roadways.

THE MARSHLANDS

LOWER DON SQUARE

THE LOWER DON MEANDER

THE PENINSULA

RECREATIONAL VALLEY

THE OUTLOOK

CENTRAL PORTLANDS

Site plan

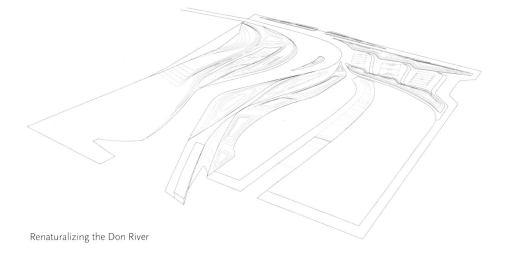

Renaturalizing the Don River

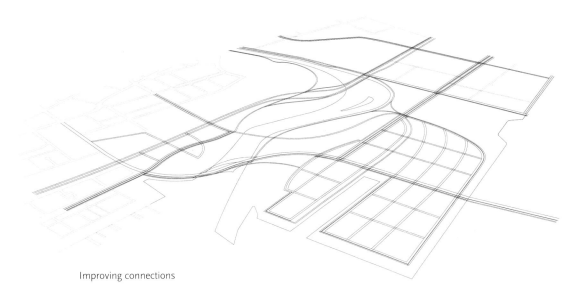

Improving connections

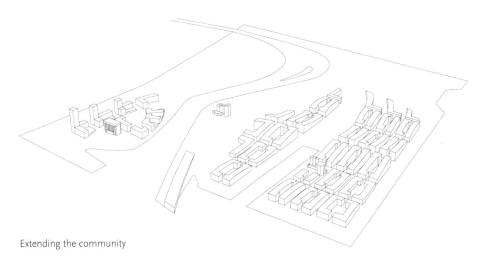

Extending the community

Perspective diagrams

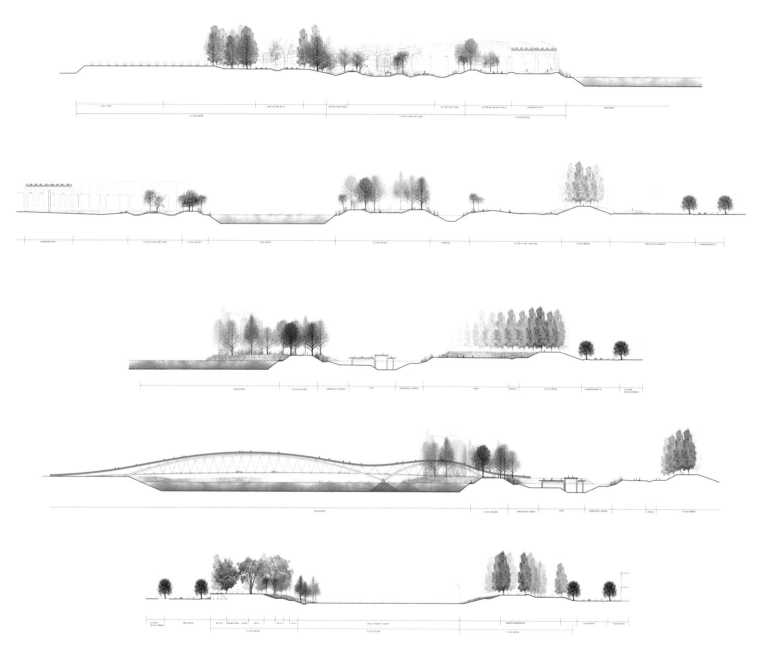

Sections

MASDAR CITY CENTER

Abu Dhabi, United Arab Emirates   2014

The construction of this plaza, which began in 2009 and is estimated to end in 2014, is part of the Masdar City master plan, under commission to Foster and Partners. It is considered one of the most sustainable developments in recent history.

LAVA was inspired by cities like Rome, Athens, and Florence, to locate a plaza or forum at the very heart of an urban fabric. In this case, given Abu Dhabi's dry climate, the planners refer to this project as the "oasis of the future." The design is centered around three key goals:

1. To demonstrate the benefits of renewable technologies in an architectural environment that is modern and iconic.
2. To have the space use renewable energy 24 hours a day and 365 days a year.
3. To have the space serve as a hub for dynamic social activity for its new community. This central hub will feature a hotel, a convention center, and retail and entertainment facilities.

The environmental parameters of the project have the aim of reducing energy demand as much as possible by applying a variety of means: specially designed parasols that store energy; cross-ventilation; cooling mist; surfaces with high thermal mass; and brise-soleil and intelligent facades for all of the buildings in the project. The plaza also features a sensor and signage system that turns on and off depending on pedestrian flow.

The project complies with the requirements set out by Estidama, a pilot standard used according to the Plan Abu Dhabi 2030, which establishes a building methodology and serves to manage buildings and communities as sustainably as possible. The USGBC LEED platinum certification was also taken as a sign to mark its progress in sustainability. The result is a project that consumes 80% less than a conventional development and is free from CO_2 emissions.

ARCHITECT
LAVA – Laboratory for Visionary Architecture

CLIENT
Abu Dhabi Future Energy Company (ADFEC)

COLLABORATORS
Bob Nation/Kann Finch Group, Arup Sydney, SL Rasch, Transsolar, EDAW

TOTAL SURFACE AREA
Approx. 1,077,000 sq ft

COST
Approx. USD 177,650,000

CERTIFICATION
Estidama Abu Dhabi (prototype stage), USGBC LEED platinum (planning stage)

PROGRAM
Public plaza, hotel, convention center, residential, entertainment, and retail space

Renderings © MIR, Atelier Illume

The "Petals from Heaven" provide cooling and shade, depending on the time of day. The facades of the surrounding buildings, which include the hotel and convention center, were designed to respond to solar angles and intensity.

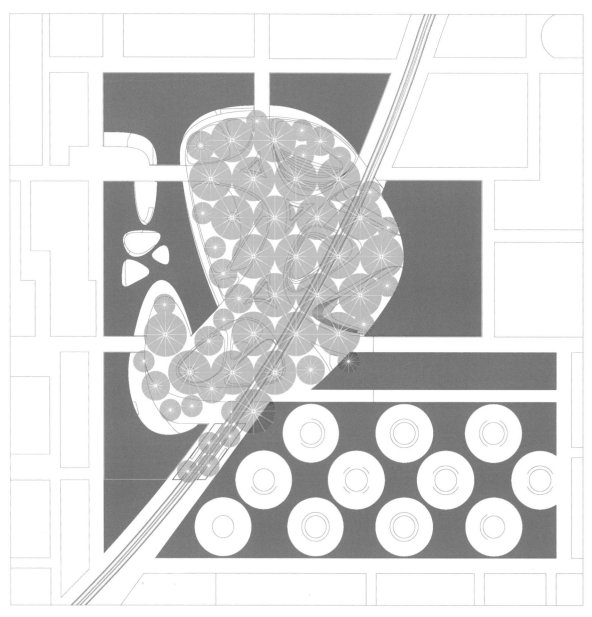

Ground plan

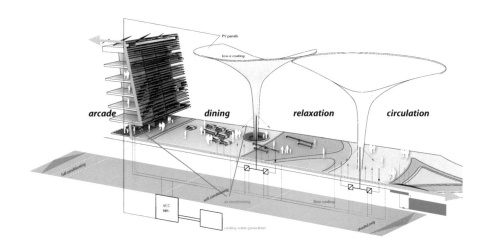

arcade   *dining*   *relaxation*   *circulation*

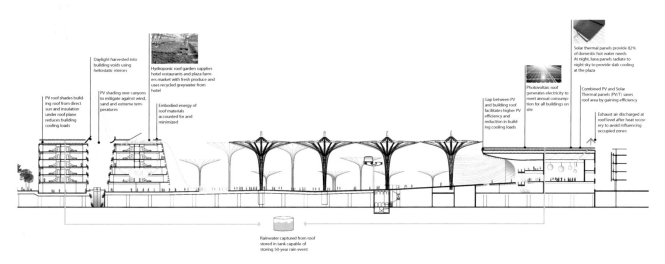

Diagram and section with environmental features

The "Petals from Heaven" are designed to open during daylight hours to provide shade while also capturing energy. They close at night and release the stored heat. They also adjust their angles to give shade depending on the position of the sun.

section 02

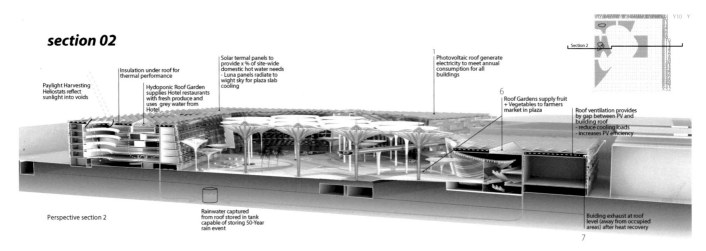

Paylight Harvesting Heliostats reflect sunlight into voids

Insulation under roof for thermal performance

Hydoponic Roof Garden supplies Hotel restaurants with fresh produce and uses grey water from Hotel

Solar termal panels to provide x % of site-wide domestic hot water needs
- Luna panels radiate to wight sky for plaza slab cooling

Photovoltaic roof generate electricity to meet annual consumption for all buildings

Roof Gardens supply fruit + Vegetables to farmers market in plaza

Roof ventilation provides by gap between PV and building roof
- reduce cooling loads
- increases PV efficiency

Perspective section 2

Rainwater captured from roof stored in tank capable of storing 50-Year rain event

Buiding exhaust at roof level (away from occupied areas) after heat recovery

Section 2

Y10 Y

6

1

7

Perspective section showing environmental features

additional solar collectors

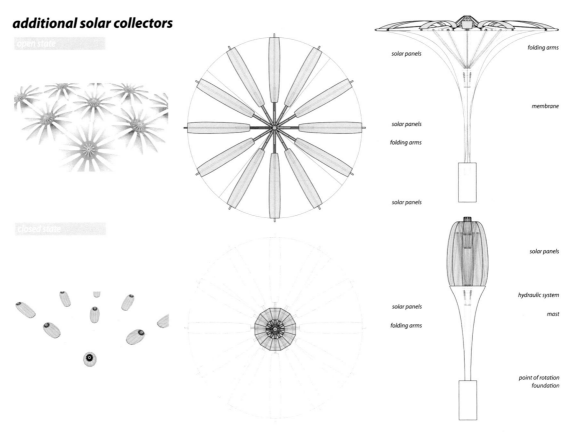

open state

closed state

solar panels

folding arms

membrane

solar panels

folding arms

solar panels

solar panels

solar panels

folding arms

hydraulic system

mast

point of rotation

foundation

Detail "Petals from Heaven"

GWANGGYO POWER CENTRE

Gwanggyo, South Korea   2011

Since the beginning of this century, South Korea has created high-density local hubs, consisting of combinations of public, retail, cultural, residential, office, and recreational spaces to revitalize urban areas. Now it is working on Gwanggyo, a city of the future, located only twenty-two miles from the Korean capital, Seoul.

Gwanggyo Power Centre is part of a master plan for this new urban hub; the other part of it is a central business district. The Power Centre is located on the south land of the master plan, surrounded by a lake and wooded hills. MVRDV is using this project to move away from the typical urban design of high-rise buildings surrounded by shopping areas, choosing instead to focus on accentuating the cultural differences between communities, which reinforces the local aspects of a community and is sustainable.

The environmentally friendly components of this project are found in its setting. MVRDV designed the new development to merge with the existing natural environment: the surrounding hills and lakes. The elements have been designed as rings. The outward expansion of the rings creates terraced areas on the outer surface, with space for plant covers and water-capturing systems.

The merging of the landscape and the high-rise design is manifest in a vertical park that improves the interior climate and cross-ventilation of the future urban core of the city, preventing excessive consumption of energy and water. The result is a design for dense urban development with a marked emphasis on green, which will form part of a new town for seventy-seven thousand inhabitants in Gwanggyo.

ARCHITECT
MVRDV

CLIENT
Daewoon Consortium and DA Group

COLLABORATORS
Arup (engineering), DA Group

TOTAL SURFACE AREA
6,500,000 sq ft

PROGRAM
Industrial, office, parking, and recreational spaces

Renderings © MVRDV

The radial layout of new buildings and biological corridors between them is designed to satisfy the project's needs for businesses while integrating the project with its surroundings and improving air quality within the buildings.

Section

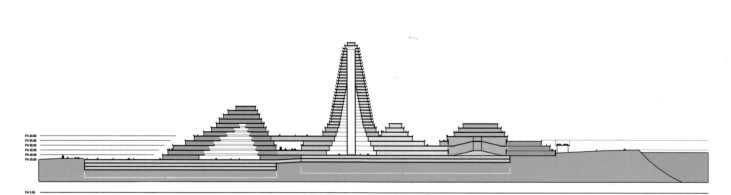

Study of building types

ZIRA ISLAND

Baku, Azerbaijan   2018

This project has been planned for Baku, in Azerbaijan, a Eurasian republic that belonged to the former Soviet Union until the 1990s. The master plan is for 10,764,000 sq ft, comprising mixed-use spaces (recreation, culture, and residential) on the waters of the Caspian Sea.

It aims to create a community with private tourist resorts, three hundred villas, and business services. Despite the monumental scale of the project, the development project aims to respect the natural environment.

The design of the buildings is based on the seven famous peaks of Azerbaijan, giving form to seven complex buildings with shapes rooted in the geometry of each mountain.

The island is designed to be self-sufficient in water and power so that it will be a carbon-neutral development.

Other environmental aspects included in the master plan are:
- The buildings will be heated and cooled by connecting heat pumps with the Caspian Sea, together with thermal solar and photovoltaic panels.
- Wastewater and rainwater will be collected, treated, and reused for watering.
- Zira Island benefits from the plentiful winds that blow in the Baku area. The project will be fed power from an offshore wind farm.

The mountains are expected to create biotopes and ecological niches, in addition to serving as a heat drain and water storage.

ARCHITECT
BIG

CLIENT
Avrositi Holding

COLLABORATORS
Ramboll (engineering)

TOTAL SURFACE AREA
10,764,000 sq ft

COST
USD 5 trillion

PROGRAM
Carbon-neutral master plan

Renderings © BIG, Ramboll Group

Located on the Bay of Baku, the complex is planned
to be carbon neutral, similar to other ecological urban
developments such as Masdar City in Abu Dhabi and
Dongtan in China.

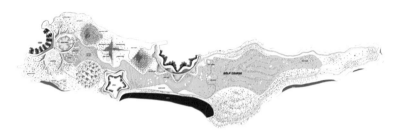

Ground plan

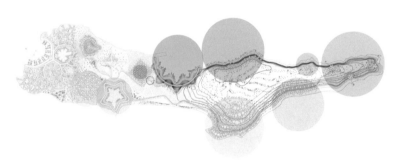

Plan showing areas for action

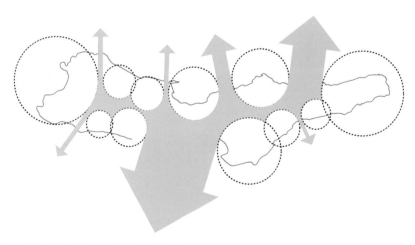

Plan with radius of influence of the public green space

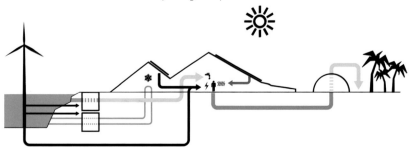

Energy and water circulation cycle chart

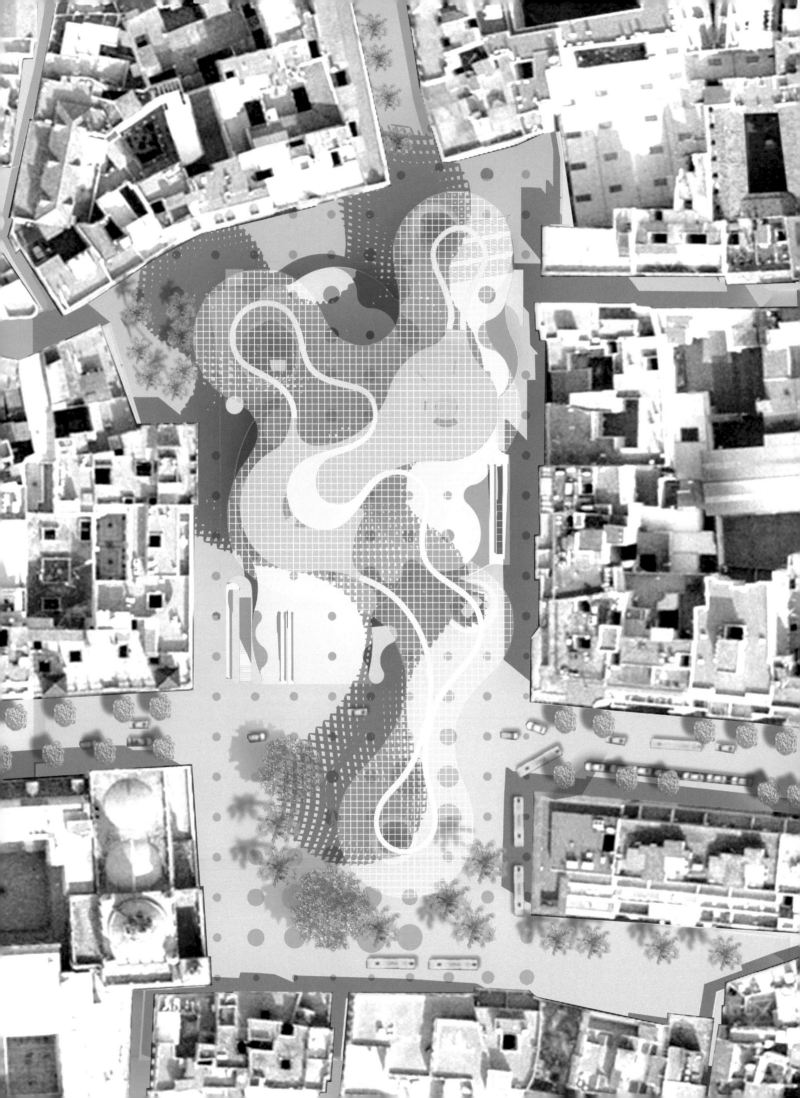

METROPOL PARASOL

Seville, Spain 2010

Metropol Parasol is a project to redesign the public space in Seville's Plaza de la Encarnación. The architect's aim is to turn it into a new contemporary hub set in the urban fabric of Seville's historic quarter.

The design of the project, built between 2005 and 2010, won the 2005 Bronze Holcim Award for sustainable construction in Europe. The foundations were completed in 2008 and the construction of the parasols has been in progress since 2009.

The new space combines references to the site's historic past with areas for leisure and commerce, and it will soon feature an archaeological space, a farmers' market, an elevated plaza, and restaurants and outdoor cafés protected from the sun by concrete parasols, with a panorama deck on top of one of the parasols.

The parasols rise from the archaeological zone, now turned into a contemporary landmark. The entrance to the museum, which is in the basement, and to the rooftop deck is through the columns.

The project aimed to respond to the needs of form and space, giving less consideration to materials; however, the design team did decide to use polyurethane-coated timber beams. The timber is PEFC-certified, this being part of a system of sustainable planting certifications managed by the forestry industry, in this case by the Finnish Forest Council of Certification. The polyurethane coating on the timber used in the parasols makes them self-cleaning and maintenance free for twenty to twenty-five years. The timber is also reinforced with steel for durability.

Aside from the shade created by the parasols, interior fountains and plants also help to create a pleasant atmosphere protected from the intense heat of a Seville summer.

ARCHITECT
J. Mayer H. Architects

CLIENT
City of Sevilla and Sacyr

COLLABORATORS
Dirk Blomeyer (management consultant), ARUP GmbH (engineering)

TOTAL SURFACE AREA
200,000 sq ft

COST
USD 81,000,000

PROGRAM
Remodeling of a public square

Photography © J. Mayer H. Architects

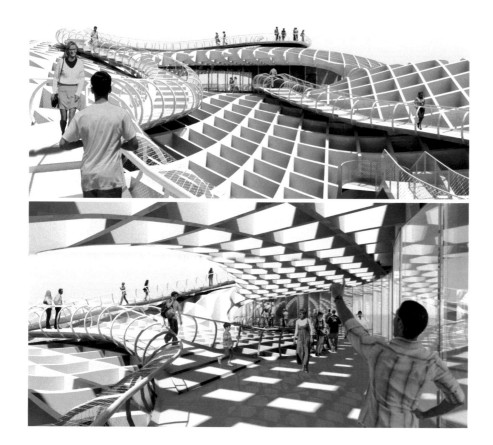

This new urban space was adapted to its climate
by incorporating a series of iconic parasols that
create shade and while serving as a transit hub or a
meeting place enhanced by the range of cultural and
gastronomic possibilities the area offers.

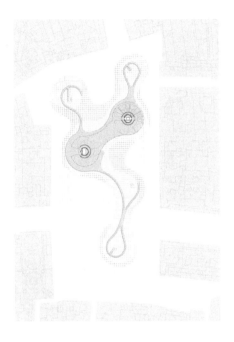

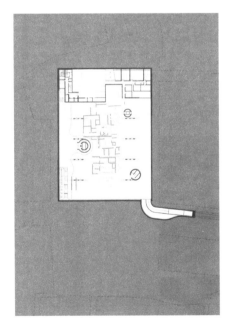
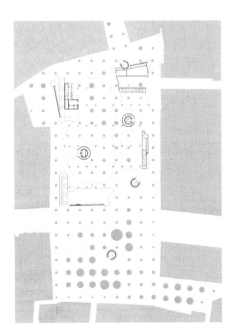

Project plans

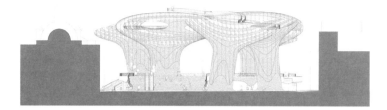

Side elevation

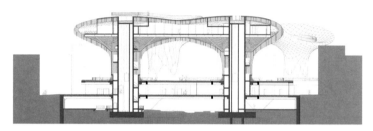

Cross-section

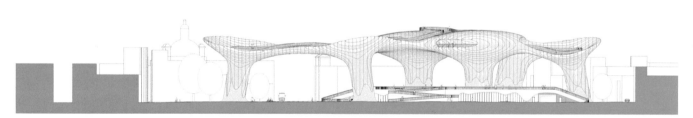

Longitudinal elevation

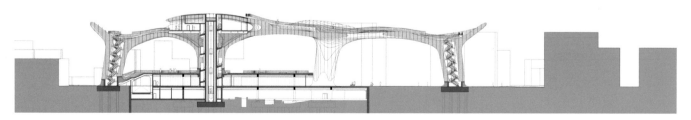

Longitudinal section

VALDESPARTERA ECOCITY

Zaragoza, Spain   2002

This new district featured bioclimatic criteria in its construction, with the purpose of achieving energy savings and environmental comfort.

The apartment blocks have a south-facing design to favor solar capture. All of the apartments have cross-ventilation.

Screens have been positioned to protect against the prevailing winds, reducing their effect, and to prevent heat loss in winter.

Secondary rooms such as bathrooms and utility rooms are located on the north side, serving to insulate living spaces. Their facades have small openings to enable light to enter and to provide ventilation. They also have thermal insulation, reducing heat loss by between 20% and 50%.

The south-facing facades feature glazed expanses and glass-encased balconies that act as greenhouses, making them warmer at night and cooler during the day. There are also passive systems, such as eaves and overhangs above windows to provide shade in summer.

The roofs are flat and hold solar thermal panels that cover 30%–50% of the yearly requirement for hot water in the apartments.

Thermo-clay ceramic bricks separate the interiors from the glassed balconies to optimize heat absorption. Ventilated facades also improve energy performance.

The waste-collection system is automated. Native plant species abound, and deciduous varieties have been planted to provide shade in summer and let sun through in winter.

ARCHITECT
Ramón Betrán Abadía/Technical Services of the Zaragoza City Council Planning Department

CLIENT
Zaragoza City Council

HABITABLE SURFACE AREA
600 acres

COST
USD 183,500,000

ENERGY CONSUMPTION
1.2–1.6 kWh/sq ft/year (residential energy use in winter)

PROGRAM
9,687-unit residential development with 97% subsidized low-cost housing

Photography © Javier Chóliz Frutos

The plan for this development is included in the
RENAISSANCE project under the Concerto initiative
of the European Union's Directorate-General for
Transport and Energy, and comprises 9,687 homes,
plus retail, office, services, and green space.

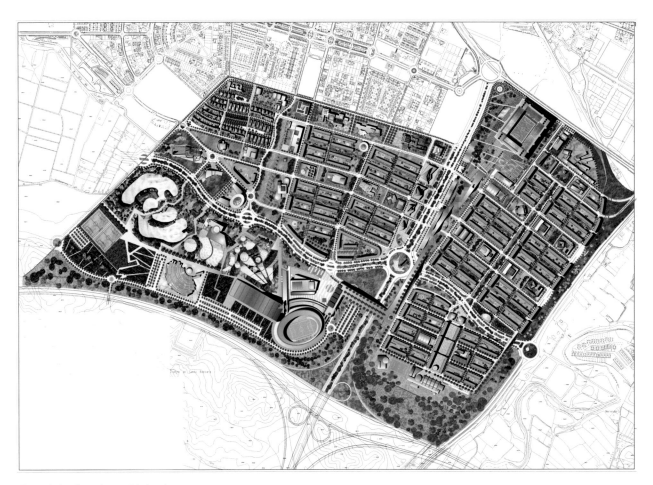

Ground plan from the partial site plan

The use of timber produced by the Spanish forestry industry was recommended for this project. Wood joinery has a certificate of origin, showing it was sourced from sustainable forests.

The Valdespartera program is a leader in green space design, with its respect for the filtering capacity of soil, moderated traffic, balance between functions, and thoughtful building design.

Photographs of the model

Glossary

Bioclimatic architecture
Construction that takes into account the climatic conditions and that makes use of available resources (sun, vegetation, rain, wind) to reduce environmental impact and energy consumption.

Brise-soleil
Screen, usually louvered, integrated into the facade of a building to protect the windows from direct sunlight.

Carbon neutral
Property whereby the balance between the carbon emissions and those sequestered or offset is equal to zero. This normally applies to construction, transportation, industrial processes, and energy production.

Cellulose insulation
Insulating material obtained from recycled newspaper. It has hygroscopic qualities, high mechanical strength and is fire-retardant.

CO_2 level control
Controlled registration and regulation of pollutant emissions of one of the gases responsible for the greenhouse effect (GHE).

Cross-ventilation
Fresh air flow generated between the hot and cold part of a building. This system is only suitable for moderate climates.

Double-height
Refers to a ceiling that is twice as high as a normal ceiling.

Ecological Cork
Cork from the sustainable exploitation of cork oak.

Emissivity
This is the proportion of thermal radiation released from a surface or object due to a given temperature difference.

Energy self-sufficiency
Ability to generate power from renewable energy equal to or more than that required for the normal operation of a building.

Forest Stewardship Council (FSC)
International certificate that guarantees consumers that forest products come from forests harvested under an economically viable, socially beneficial, and environmentally responsible forest management policy.

Formaldehyde-free MDF
Chipboard made from wood fibers combined with resins by high pressure and heat, and then dried to reach a standard density. Resins should not release formaldehyde, as it is a highly volatile and highly flammable chemical.

Fossil fuel
A mixture of mineralized organic compounds that are extracted from the subsoil for the purpose of producing energy by combustion. Coal, petrol, and natural gas are considered to be fossil fuels.

Geothermal energy source
Energy obtained by harnessing the heat inside the Earth.

Gray water recycling
The reuse of water from personal care facilities (shower and sink), kitchen, and household cleaning, through previous treatment.

Greenhouse effect
Phenomenon whereby certain gases retain some of the energy that the soil emits due to solar radiation. Carbon dioxide (CO_2) and methane from human economic activity are two of the main causes.

Heat-recovery ventilation system (HRV)
Ventilation system that uses counterflow heat between the inlet and outlet air flow. The heat-recovery ventilator allows for the efficient renewal of interior air without wasting interior heat, and it can represent energy savings of 15%–30%.

Insulated glazing
Glass with air chambers that reduces losses due to thermal bridging and poor air tightness. It is also known as double glazing or chamber glass.

Insulation
Capacity of material to prevent the passage of heat by conduction. It is measured in $m^2 \cdot K/W$.

Low-VOC paints
Water-based paint or paint without solvent. It has a low emission of volatile organic compounds, which are precursors of the tropospheric ozone and deplete the stratospheric ozone.

Modular building system
Construction system based on the assembly of prefabricated modular units, permitting everything from the creation of small architectural spaces to multiuse buildings.

Photovoltaic panel
Panel that uses the energy from sunlight, consisting of cells that convert light into electricity.

Radiant floor heating
Installation consisting of a cross-linked polyethylene pipe that distributes heat or cold through a fluid. It is an invisible type of heating and it generates less airborne dust and provides a stable temperature.

Rainwater collection
Use of rainwater through downspouts and an underground water-collection tank.

Regulable louvers
Louvers that can be adjusted, so that there are gaps that favor air flow and prevent the entry of light, rain, or snow. The final position influences the building's interior temperature.

Solar gain
The control of direct solar radiation that reaches the interior of a building, through the use of windows, skylights, shutters, or the provision of thermal mass floors, which retain heat.

Solar thermal panels
Panel designed to collect heat from the sun and turn it into thermal energy. The heat is transferred to a fluid to be heated, which can be either tap water or the home's hydraulic heating system.

Sunshade
Any of several solar control systems consisting of horizontal or vertical elements fixed and arranged with a certain inclination to protect a window from direct sunlight.

Thermal comfort model
Expresses the satisfaction of a person with the surrounding thermal environment.

Thermal mass
This is the potential capacity of a body or system to store heat. Water walls, concrete floors, and adobe walls are good examples.

Upcycling
This is the process of converting waste or useless objects into new objects of better quality or a higher value.

Venturi effect
Physical process through which the pressure of a moving fluid within a closed conduit is reduced after passing through a constricted section of pipe. In a building this effect produces the renewal of the interior air.

Wind turbine
Electric generator driven by a wind-powered turbine.

Main International Environmental Certification Programs

LEED – The Leadership in Energy and Environmental Design
Creation: 1993
Management: US Green Building Council
Building types: commercial and residential
Ratings: Certified, Silver, Gold, and Platinum
Territories: USA, Canada, Brazil, Mexico, and India
www.usgbc.org/LEED

Green Star
Creation: 2003
Management: Green Building Council Australia
Building types: commercial offices, retail centers, schools, universities, multi-unit residential dwellings, industrial facilities, and public buildings.
Ratings: 4 Star Green Star, 5 Star Green Star, 6 Star Green Star
Territories: Australia
www.gbca.org.au/green-star

BREEAM – BRE Environmental Assessment Method
Creation: 1990
Management: BRE Global
Building types: education, retail, offices, prisons, industrial, healthcare, courts, and residential
Ratings: Pass, Good, Very Good, Excellent, and Outstanding
Territories: UK, Europe, and Gulf region
www.breeam.org

CASBEE – Comprehensive Assessment System for Built Environment Efficiency
Creation: 2001
Management: Japan Sustainable Building Consortium (JSBC)
Building types: new construction, existing building, renovation, and urban development
Ratings: C (poor), class B-, class B+, class A, and class S (excellent)
Territories: Japan
www.ibec.or.jp/CASBEE/english/

PassivHaus
Creation: 1991
Management: Passivhaus Institut
Building types: residential and nonresidential
Territories: Germany, Switzerland, Austria, France, Italy, and Spain
www.passiv.de

MINERGIE®
Creation: 1998
Management: MINERGIE®
Building types: buildings (residential, institutional, schools, commercial, industrial, swimming pools, and hospitals), products, and services
Ratings: Minergie, Minergie-P, Minergie-Eco
Territories: Switzerland, Austria, Luxembourg, Lichtenstein, Germany, France, Italy, and USA
www.minergie.com

Others:

Canada, USA
Green Globes; www.greenglobes.com

Australia
Nabers; www.nabers.com.au

Hong Kong
BEAM; www.hk-beam.org.hk

India
GRIHA; www.grihaindia.org

Singapore
BCA Green Mark;
www.bca.gov.sg/GreenMark/green_mark_buildings.html

France
Effinergie; www.effinergie.org

Germany
DGNB; www.dgnb.de

Italy
Protocollo Itaca; www.itaca.org

Directory

2012Architecten
Rotterdam, Netherlands
www.2012architecten.nl

Adam Kalkin/Quik Build
Bernardsville, NJ, USA
www.quik-build.com

Agence Paysages
Lille, France
www.lascop-paysages.com

Alonso, Balaguer y Arquitectos Asociados
Esplugues de Llobregat, Spain
www.alonsobalaguer.com

Altius Architecture
Toronto, ON, Canada
www.altius.net

Architekturbüro Reinberg
Vienna, Austria
www.reinberg.net

Arkitektfirmaet C.F. Møller
Århus, Denmark
www.cfmoller.com

Atelier Dreiseitl
Überlingen, Germany
www.dreiseitl.com

Atelier du Pont
Paris, France
www.atelierdupont.fr

Balmori Associates
New York, NY, USA
www.balmori.com

Bark Design
Noosa Heads, Australia
www.barkdesign.com.au

Behnisch Architekten
Stuttgart, Germany
www.behnisch.com

BIG – Bjarke Ingels Group
Copenhagen, Denmark
www.big.dk

Bruno Stagno
San José, Costa Rica
www.brunostagno.info

BVN Architecture
Melbourne, Australia
www.bvn.com.au

Cass Calder Smith Architecture
San Francisco, CA, USA
www.ccs-architecture.com

Charles Barclay Architects
London, United Kingdom
www.cbarchitects.co.uk

Dan Rockhill/Rockhill + Associates
Lecompton, KS, USA
www.rockhillandassociates.com

David Baker + Partners Architects
San Francisco, CA, USA
www.dbarchitect.com

DeMaria Design Associates
Manhattan Beach, CA, USA
www.demariadesign.com

Denton Corker Marshall
Melbourne, Australia
www.dentoncorkermarshall.com.au

Dietrich Schwarz
Zürich, Switzerland
www.glassx.ch

Diller Scofidio + Renfro
New York, NY, USA
www.dillerscofidio.com

Ecosistema Urbano
Madrid, Spain
www.ecosistemaurbano.com

Édouard François
Paris, France
www.edouardfrancois.com

Equip d'Arquitectura Pich-Aguilera
Barcelona, Spain
www.picharchitects.com

FXFOWLE Architects
New York, NY, USA
www.fxfowle.com

G56
Barcelona, Spain
www.g56.com

Gray Puksand
Melbourne, Australia
www.graypuksand.com.au

Guillermo Hevia/GH + A
Santiago, Chile
www.guillermohevia.cl

Hastings Architecture Associates
Nashville, TN, USA
www.haa.us

Hérault Arnod Architectes
Grenoble, France
www.herault-arnod.fr

**Hobby A. Schuster & Maul,
Gerold Peham/Nomadhome Trading**
Seekirchen, Austria
www.nomadhome.com

Holz Box
Innsbruck, Austria
www.holzbox.at

Hughes Condon Marler Architects
Vancouver, BC, Canada
www.hcma.ca

J. Mayer H. Architects
Berlin, Germany
www.jmayerh.de

James Corner Field Operations
New York, NY, USA
www.fieldoperations.net

James & Mau
Madrid, Spain
www.jamesandmau.com

Jennifer Siegal/Office of Mobile Design
Venice, CA, USA
www.designmobile.com

Jestico + Whiles
London, United Kingdom
www.jesticowhiles.com

Kuwabara Payne McKenna Blumberg Architects
Toronto, ON, Canada
www.kpmbarchitects.com

LAVA – Laboratory for Visionary Architecture
Sttutgart, Germany
www.l-a-v-a.net

LOOK Architects
Singapore, Republic of Singapore
www.lookarchitects.com.sg

Luca Lancini
Barcelona, Spain
www.lucalancini.com

Manuel Ruisánchez/Ruisánchez Arquitectes
Barcelona, Spain
www.ruisanchez.net

Marc Opdebeeck/Modelmo Architecte
Brussels, Belgium
www.modelmo.be

Mario Cucinella Architects
Bologna, Italy
www.mcarchitects.it

Marmol Radziner Prefab
Los Angeles, CA, USA
www.marmolradzinerprefab.com

McGregor Coxall
Sydney, Australia
www.mcgregorcoxall.com

Mithun
Seattle, WA, USA
www.mithun.com

Mizien Arquitectura
Barcelona, Spain
www.mizien.com

MVRDV
Rotterdam, Netherlands
www.mvrdv.nl

Patkau Architects
Vancouver, BC, Canada
www.patkau.ca

Ramón Betrán Abadía/Servicios técnicos de urbanismo del Ayuntamiento de Zaragoza
Zaragoza, Spain
www.zaragoza.es

RAU
Amsterdam, Netherlands
www.rau.eu

Renzo Piano Building Workshop
Genoa, Italy
www.rpbw.com

Rolf Disch SolarArchitektur
Freiburg, Germany
www.rolfdisch.de

Rongen Architekten
Wassenberg, Germany
www.rongen-architekten.de

RSHP – Rogers, Stirk, Harbour + Partners
London, United Kingdom
www.richardrogers.co.uk

Ruiz-Larrea & Asociados
Madrid, Spain
www.ruizlarrea.com

Samyn and Partners architects & engineers
Brussels, Belgium
www.samynandpartners.be

Solares Architecture
Toronto, ON, Canada
www.solares.ca

Studio 804
Lawrence, KS, USA
www.studio804.com

Takenaka Corporation
Tokyo, Japan
www.takenaka.co.jp

Taketo Shimohigoshi/A.A.E.
Tokyo, Japan
www.aae.jp

The High Line
New York, NY, USA
www.thehighline.org

Toyo Ito & Associates Architects
Tokyo, Japan
www.toyo-ito.co.jp

Trauner.Strobl.Bach Architekten Ziviltechniker
Salzburg, Austria
www.tsb-architekten.com

Triptyque Architecture
Paris, France
www.triptyque.com

Ventura Trindade Arquitectos
Lisbon, Portugal
www.venturatrindade.com

Weiss/Manfredi
New York, NY, USA
www.weissmanfredi.com

WOHA Designs
Singapore, Republic of Singapore
www.wohadesigns.com

412179

412179